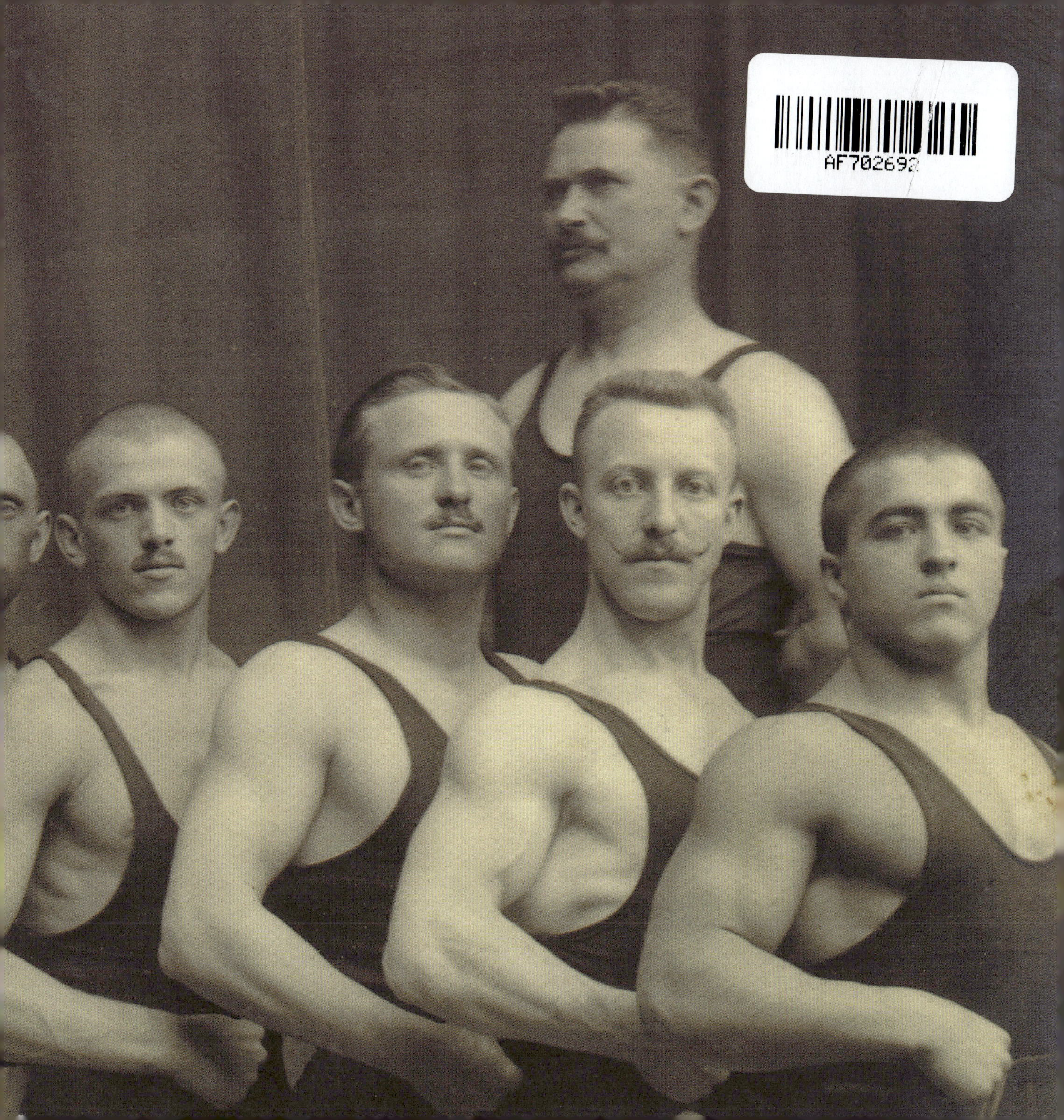

Strong Man

Vintage Photos of a Masculine Icon

Edited and with an Introduction by

Robert Mainardi

Foreword by Jules Bacon
Mr. America 1943

Council Oak Books

San Francisco/Tulsa

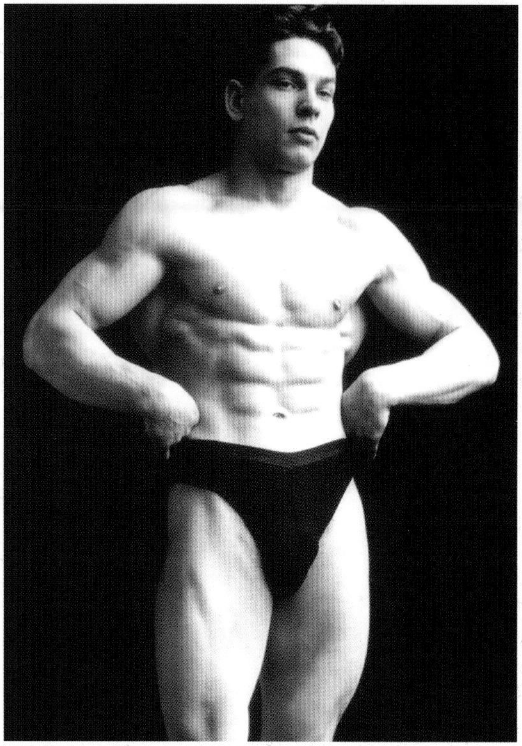

Foreword

The book you hold in your hands offers a unique glimpse into the world of bodybuilding and physical culture, which has been both my home and career for over sixty years. I began weight training in 1937 at the age of twenty and won my first title, Mr. Philadelphia, in 1940. Training hard for the 1941 Mr. America contest, I was encouraged and satisfied when I came in second place to the great John Grimek. This was an exciting time: I spent most of 1942 visiting Philadelphia schools with Jesse Owens, the Olympic champion, in the "Hail America" Program sponsored by Eleanor Roosevelt as part of the war effort. Taking a leave from my job at the York Barbell Company in York, Pennsylvania, I traveled out to California to train for the 1943 Mr. America contest, which I had the great thrill of winning, proudly joining an elite list of athletes, some of whom are pictured in this book.

I subsequently did a lot of traveling with my friend Bob Hoffman, the head of York Barbell and publisher of the pioneering magazine *Strength and Health*. Through my association with Bob I met many of the great names in the sport of bodybuilding: Sig Klein, Otto Arco, Charles Atlas, Joe Bonomo and the man from whom I'd bought my first set of barbells, Earle Liederman. At the legendary Yarick's Gym in California I had the pleasure of getting to know Steve Reeves (later to be immortalized on the screen as *Hercules*) and we became good friends. Over the years I got to spend a lot of time at Muscle Beach in Santa Monica, legendary meeting place of bodybuilders from all over the world, and there I met everyone from Bert Goodrich, the first Mr. America, to Arnold Schwarzenegger.

The photos in this nostalgic collection bring back many fond memories of the exciting events I've witnessed and the wonderful people I've met. *Strongman* beautifully recaptures the world of "barbells and physiques" I knew so well.

—JULES BACON, *Mr. America 1943*

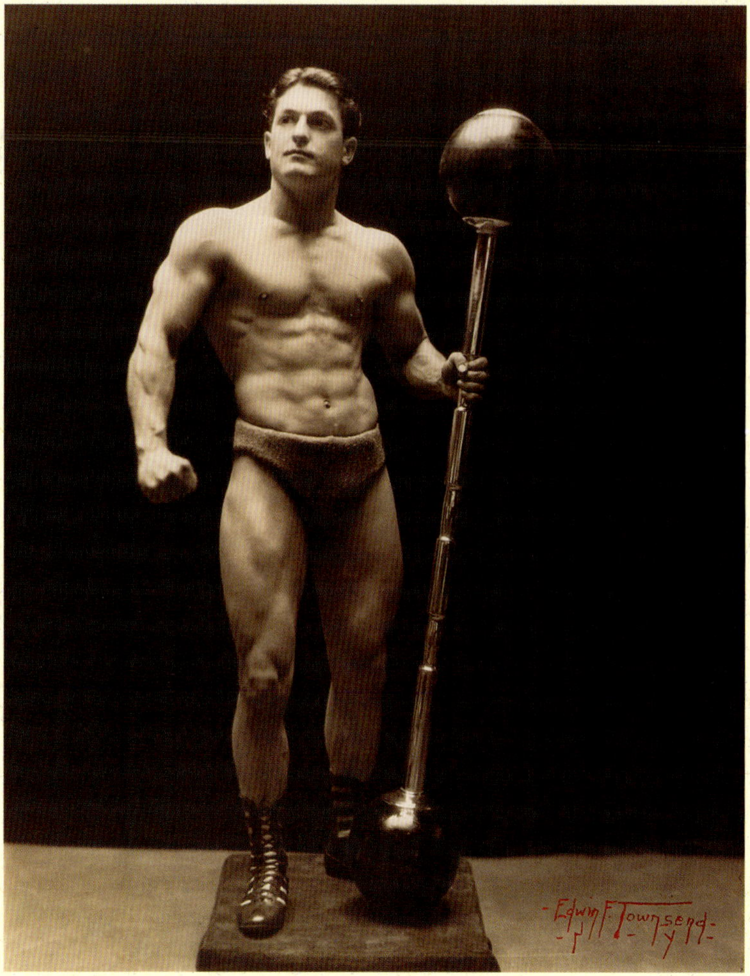

John Garon by Edwin F. Townsend.
Silverprint, c. 1915.

Introduction

It all began with the Encyclopedia Britannica. When I was seven or eight years old my father, a college professor, decided to remodel the attic of our house to make bedrooms for my older brother and me. He created a special built-in bookcase in my brother's room for the *Encyclopedia Britannica* he expected both of us to use to help us excel in our academic studies. While I'm sure we did use this intellectual resource for innumerable school projects and reports, for me it offered another attraction. I can remember spending many afternoons in the silence of my brother's bedroom while he was outside playing handball or baseball and my parents were at work or preoccupied with their own activities. In the warmth of the sunlight slanting in through the venetian blinds and painting the room with golden stripes, I'd sit on the floor and choose one of the precisely alphabetized big maroon volumes, spreading it open in my lap. Slowly I would turn the thin, smooth pages looking for pictures of naked people. Of course, these consisted largely of photographs of famous paintings and sculptures, but to me they represented the mysterious and secret world of the body. Long before understanding or experiencing the sexual attraction of the nude, I was seduced by its sensual beauty. The Elgin Marbles, the Farnese *Hercules*, Michelangelo's figures of *David* and *The Pietà* and the sculptures for the Medici Tomb, all of the smooth white marble Roman copies of lost Greek masterpieces: these were my innocent introduction to representations of the human body.

My fascination with images was further heightened by my father's collection of old magazines piled high in the unfinished storage room under the eaves of the attic. Being an amateur photographer (and inventor of a particularly good 3-D camera attachment), he had many years' worth of magazines like *Popular Photography* and *Modern Photography*, *Pageant, Fortune, Life* and many other titles. I would spend hours looking through these, sometimes surreptitiously clipping out particularly haunting images (often, but not always, nudes) and secreting them away in folders and scrapbooks, a hobby that was to become a lifelong obsession. The nudes depicted were, for the most part, "artistic studies," but here and there I discovered photos of real men (albeit in singlets or posing straps): athletes, lifeguards, wrestlers, strongmen and bodybuilders. These last were the most fascinating of all because, unlike those men whose work or sport incidentally resulted in hard, chiseled physiques, these individuals worked out specifically in order to turn their bodies into a preconceived ideal form. Looking at my scrawny boy-body in the mirror on my mother's closet door, I could only imagine there were real people who looked like works of art. But there were, and I was developing an indelible reverence not merely for the splendor of the human body (and particularly the male body) but also for the image of "the body beautiful."

Soon after this I discovered there were whole magazines devoted to just this activity of weightlifting and bodybuilding; magazines like *Strength and Health, Muscle Power* and *Iron Man* showcased men striving to look like Apollo or Hercules, and vying for titles like Mr. America and Mr. Universe. These publications featured page after page of pictures of well-built men who were proud to display their bodies like works of art while espousing the benefits of "working out" for strength, health and self-confidence. This was in the early 1950s when an interest in health foods, weightlifting and bodybuilding generally earned one the derisive labels "muscle-bound" and "crackpot." Nor did it help that one of the great purveyors of the "healthy" lifestyle was Bernarr Macfadden (p.107), publisher of the magazine *Physical Culture* from the turn of the century until the early 1950s, whose motto was "Weakness a Crime—Don't Be a Criminal" and who endorsed everything from carrot juice to nudism. I quickly came to understand that this was not a hobby for the retiring or faint of heart, just as I discovered that the sexual attractiveness of the human body could not readily be divorced from its aesthetic appeal.

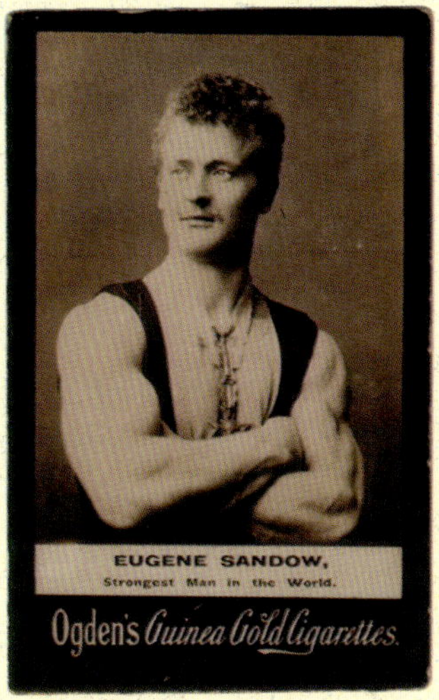

About this time a genre of "little magazines" with titles like *Adonis*, *The Body Beautiful*, *Vim* and *Trim* began to appear, including the first that I ever had the nerve to buy at a newsstand in 1957, *Fizeek*. The appeal of these magazines was overtly homoerotic, even though they featured some of the same photos of famous bodybuilders that had appeared in bodybuilding magazines for decades. These were the same images in a new context and, more than ever, I became entranced by the power and symbolism of the images themselves.

When I was about ten or twelve years old my parents discovered my stash of photo clippings and, in an obvious effort to channel my interest in a healthy direction, bought me a set of weights and a workout bench.

Eugen Sandow, Strongest Man in the World.
British cigarette card, c. 1890.

But, after a half-hearted attempt to teach myself the fundamentals of weightlifting, I quickly realized I lacked both the motivation and the interest to transform my own body. I was not athletic and no amount of daydreaming seemed likely to change that fact. What I lacked was a fundamental belief that I *could* change myself through sheer willpower. Besides, I didn't want to be Hercules; I wanted to *see* Hercules.

One summer day when I was a teenager on my way downtown to the library, the bus I was on came to a stoplight and I saw a van parked at the curb bearing a famous bodybuilding logo. I stared in amazement as Dave Draper, Mr. America 1965 and a rising star in the Weider firmament, lifted a set of weights out of the van. His California platinum blond, movie-star looks were hard to mistake in dull, gray New Jersey, not to mention his superhero body shown off in a sleeveless white T-shirt. I was too young and too shy to pull the cord, jump off the bus and race to meet one of my idols. I could only spend the rest of the day scheming how I might order more weightlifting equipment (to add to that which already sat unused in our basement) and ask that it be delivered by him. This was just another daydream, of course, yet it provided something even more valuable to me than an actual encounter with Dave Draper. I had the image of him, big and blond and flexing his muscles as he worked, imprinted in my mind. That icon became my passion.

"Cutting out paper dolls," as my partner often refers to our mutual hobby of collecting images of the male physique, is something I have done almost my whole life. It has brought me much pleasure and satisfaction. I've also learned a lot about the motivations and compulsions of the real men whose images I so admire. The old wives' tale that all men who build up their bodies do so to compensate for some deep seated feeling of inadequacy is as infrequently true as the urban legend (invented by Angelo Siciliano, aka Charles Atlas, p. 78) that they do so because some bully once kicked sand in their face. In fact, the drive to perfect one's body through exercise has always appealed to strong-willed individualists who are undeterred by skepticism and ridicule. Whether a man has simply sought to have a well-built body he could display with pride or has worked to achieve fame and recognition in the increasingly "professional" world of bodybuilding, this has always required hard work and a healthy ego.

If history suggests a recurrent societal ambivalence between body-pride and body-shame, between Greco-Roman athleticism and Victorian prudery, the twentieth century has certainly witnessed a return of the glorification of the male physique not seen since antiquity. This is largely due to the development of photography. The advent of the Herculean male didn't begin with Arnold Schwarzenegger but rather culminated with his acceptance by the general public as a figure to be admired and emulated. Almost exactly a century earlier another strongman took to the stage to seek the same kind of fortune and adulation, with unprecedented success. His name was Eugen Sandow (pp. 7, 9, 11, 37, 41, 45, 93).

Sandow, a British strongman of German extraction, was already a celebrity in Europe when he was first brought to the United States by

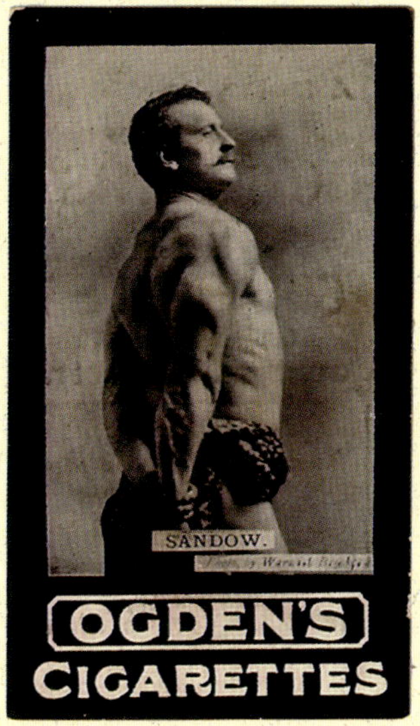

Eugen Sandow by Warwick Brookes.
British cigarette card, c. 1905.

Florenz Ziegfeld in 1893. In the world of European circus and music halls there was a long tradition of strongman acts consisting of acrobatics and hand-balancing, feats of strength and very theatrical "contests." Sandow stormed this world, quickly becoming famous not only for his strength but also for the beauty of his physique and his posing grace. He was also a shrewd businessman who published his own magazine, wrote books and marketed his own line of exercise equipment. When Ziegfeld offered him the opportunity to appear in America he took it and together they made a fortune. This was the beginning of the modern era of bodybuilding, and of the public exhibition of the male body. It was also the beginning of an ongoing debate regarding athletics vs. aesthetics, fame vs. notoriety, and health vs. excess. (Sandow's death in 1925 was erroneously attributed to his rashly lifting a wrecked car from a ditch.) None of this has changed the determination with which some men continue to push the physical envelope. After Sandow there was Atlas, who himself named bodybuilder Tony Sansone "The Most Beautiful Man in America" (p. 28); then John Grimek, twice Mr. America (p. 81), and Jules Bacon, who took the title in 1943 (p. 2); Jack LaLanne, television fitness guru (p. 32); movie *Hercules* Steve Reeves (p. 84); Hungarian immigrant and 1957 Mr. Universe Mickey Hargitay (p. 100), and hosts of others. Some became famous names while many were forgotten. Many provided us with unforgettable images, some with iconic ones.

This album offers a sampling of images, both professional and amateur, from the 1880s to the middle of the twentieth century. There are classic images by photographers famous in the genre: Hana, Sarony, Drtikol,

Townsend, Forbes, Lon and Lanza. In addition to the carefully posed "professionals" there are amazing amateur shots of men who never sought fame or adulation but whose physical beauty and pride of physique were captured by the camera in moments both serious and carefree. These pictures were kept and treasured in frames, photo albums or cigar boxes for decades, now finally reappearing here. Like all snapshots, they reveal the "real world" reverberations of an increasingly image-saturated society. What were the results of Granddad sending for that Charles Atlas course found packed away in the attic? What were those summers like, so long ago, when Dad and his buddies practiced acrobatic pyramids like the fellows they'd seen photographed at Muscle Beach? The candid image has as much to tell us as the posed.

Strongman shows the well-built next to the Herculean, the playfully athletic next to the seriously competitive, the shyly proud next to the boldly exhibitionistic. Here are men who defined their own masculinity, who trained and sculpted their bodies in pursuit of an ideal, and who embraced their physicality without shame (at least, none the camera can see). And the essence of this collection is what the camera *has* seen: images of strength unalloyed with weakness, and of inspiration unclouded by doubt. There are those who would say such images are unreal, manipulative or misleading, but for me the very joy of images lies in where they can lead us. Here is a collection of strongmen to lead us up Olympus.

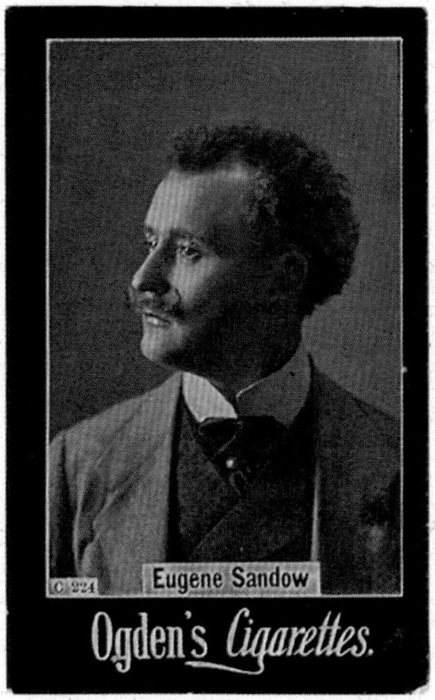

Eugen Sandow.
British cigarette card, c. 1905.

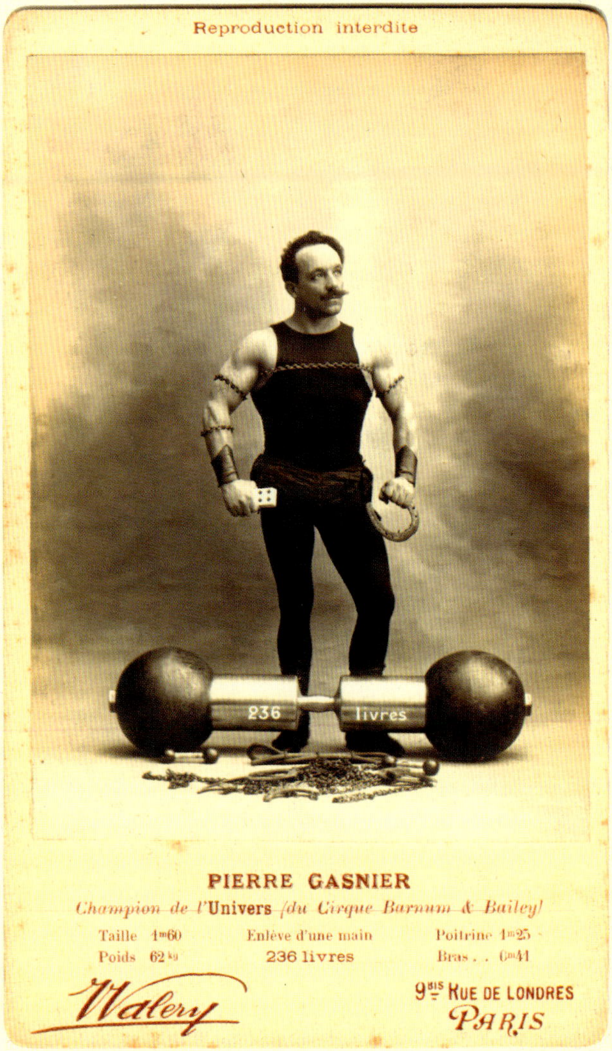

Pierre Gasnier, Champion of the Universe (Barnum & Bailey Circus) by Walery, Paris. Cabinet card, c. 1900.

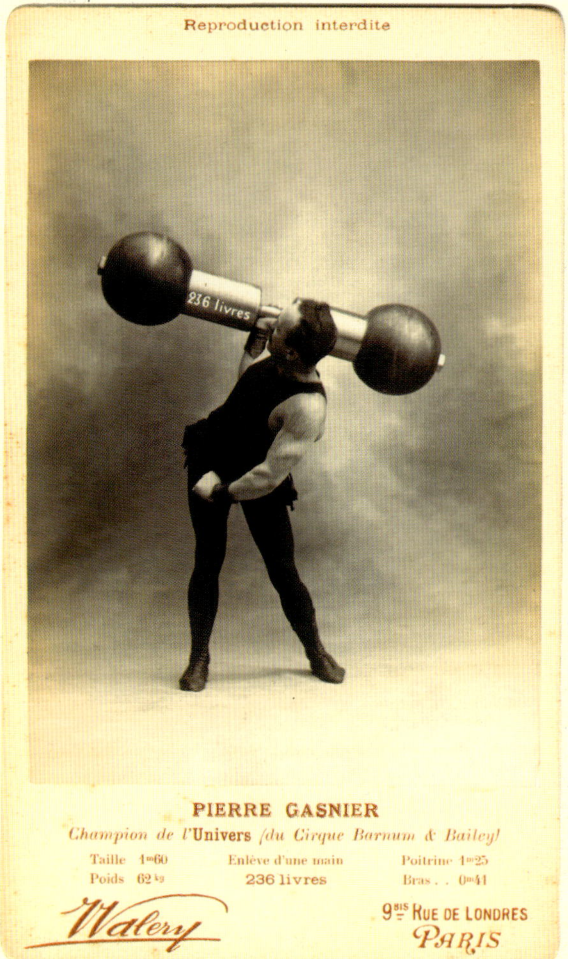
Reproduction interdite
236 livres
PIERRE GASNIER
Champion de l'Univers (du Cirque Barnum & Bailey)
Taille 1m60
Poids 62 kg
Enlève d'une main
236 livres
Poitrine 1m25
Bras . . 0m41
Walery
9bis Rue de Londres
Paris

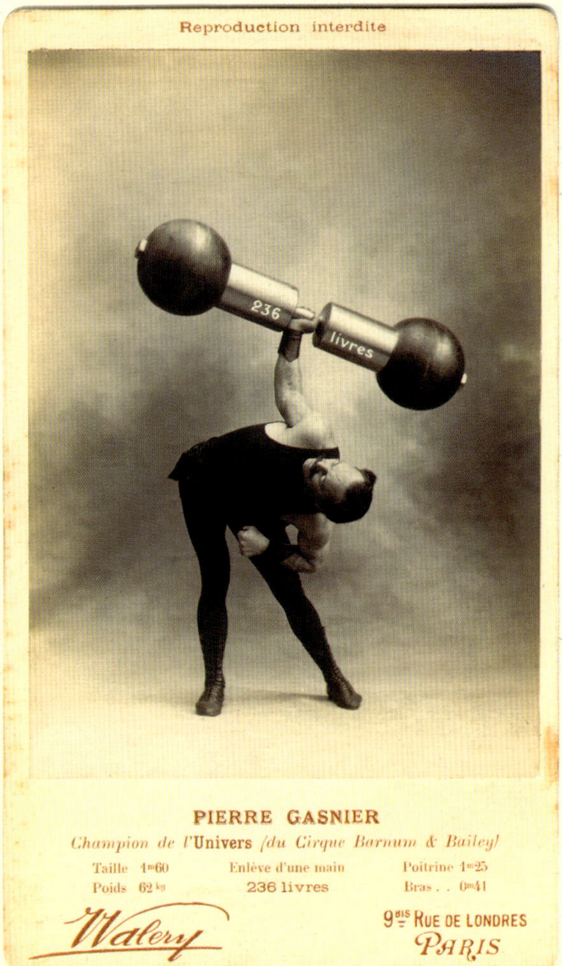
Reproduction interdite
236
livres
PIERRE GASNIER
Champion de l'Univers (du Cirque Barnum & Bailey)
Taille 1m60
Poids 62 kg
Enlève d'une main
236 livres
Poitrine 1m25
Bras . . 0m41
Walery
9bis Rue de Londres
Paris

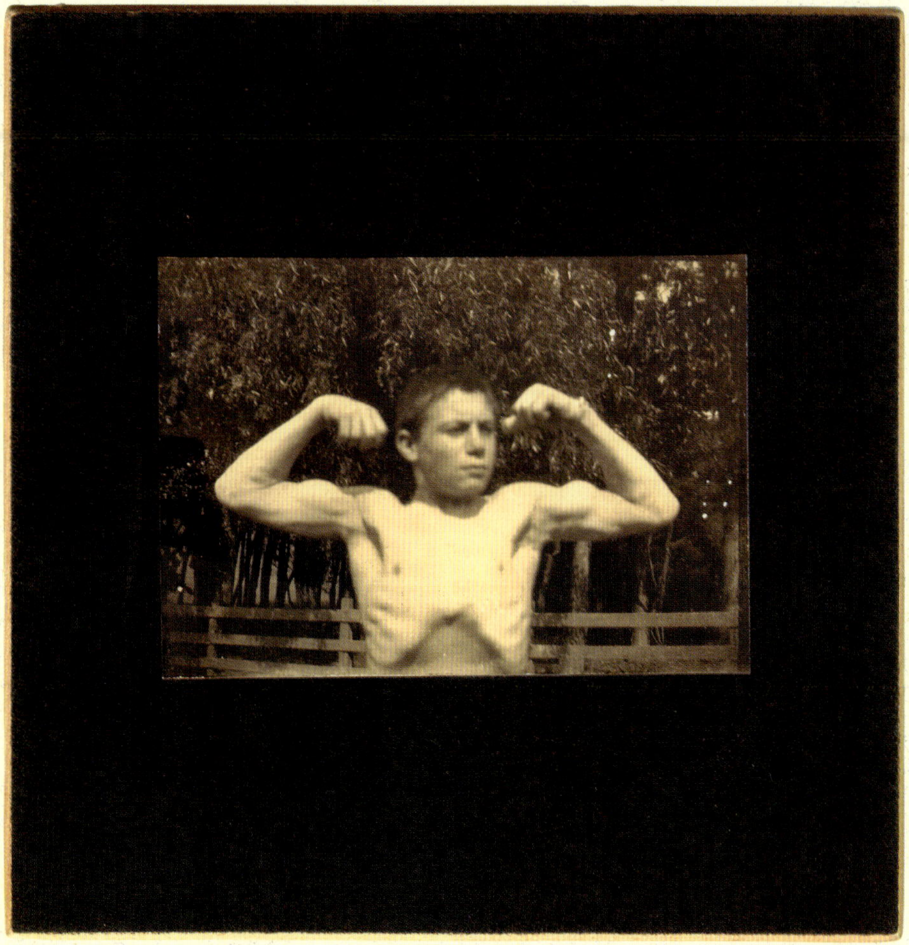

Anonymous snapshot, c. 1915.

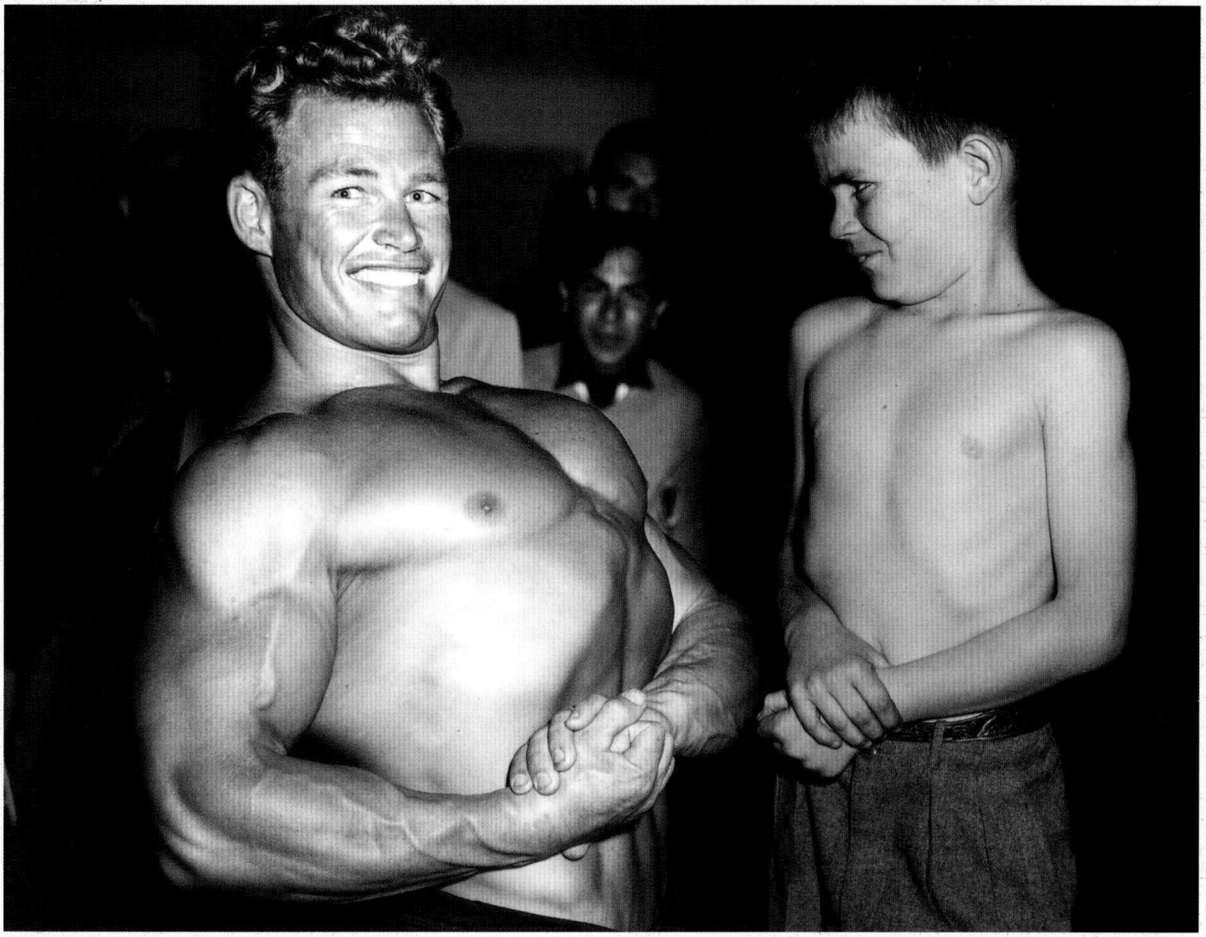

Roy Hilligen, Mr. America 1951
by Bruce Bellas. Silverprint, c. 1951.

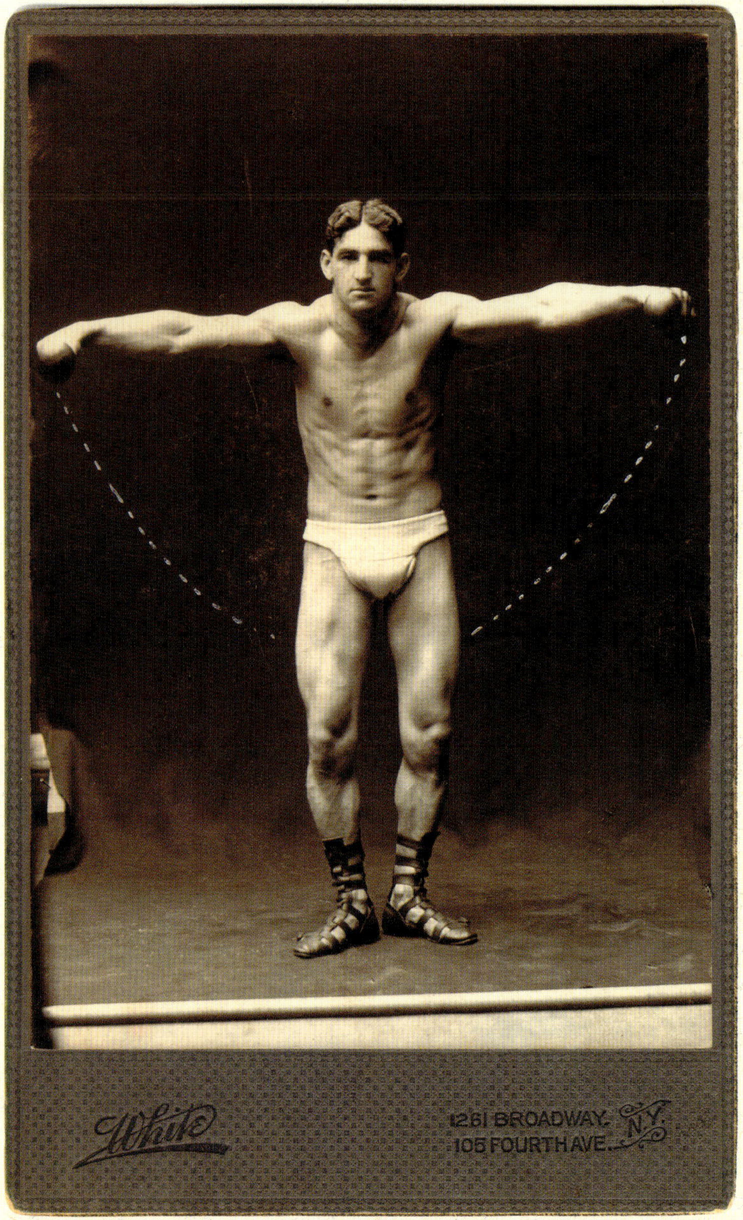

Harry Wexler by White, New York City.
Cabinet card, c. 1890.

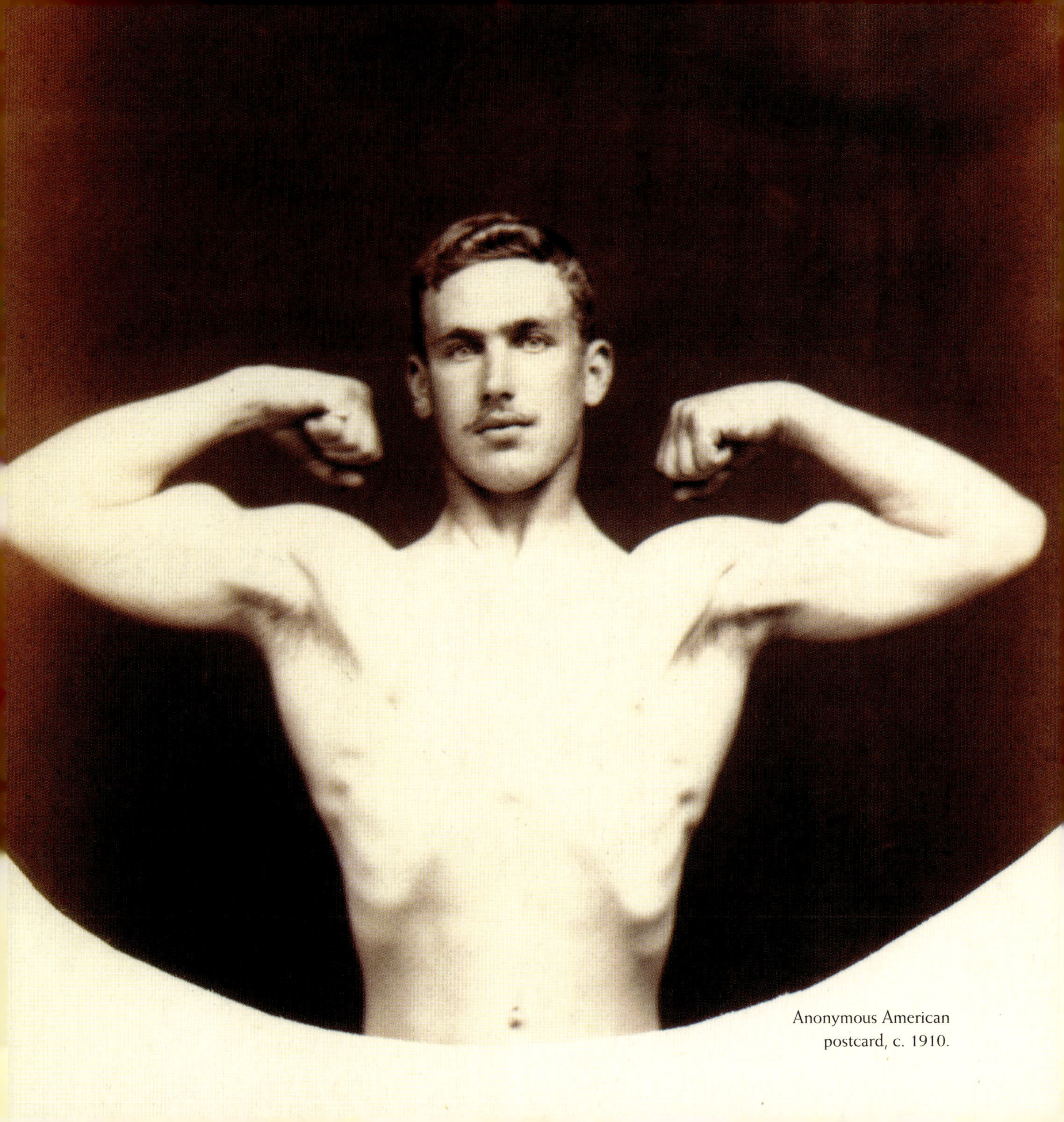

Anonymous American
postcard, c. 1910.

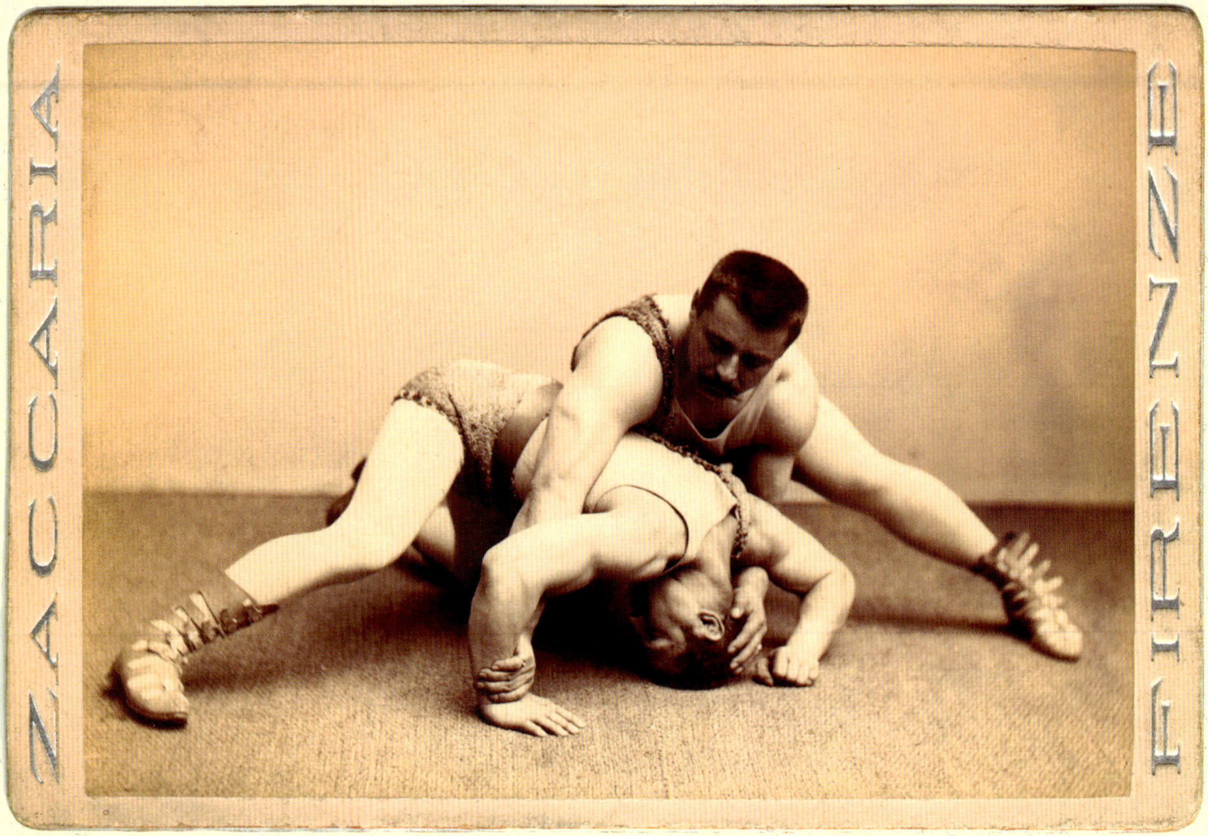

Wrestlers by Zaccaria, Florence, Italy.
Cabinet card, c. 1900.

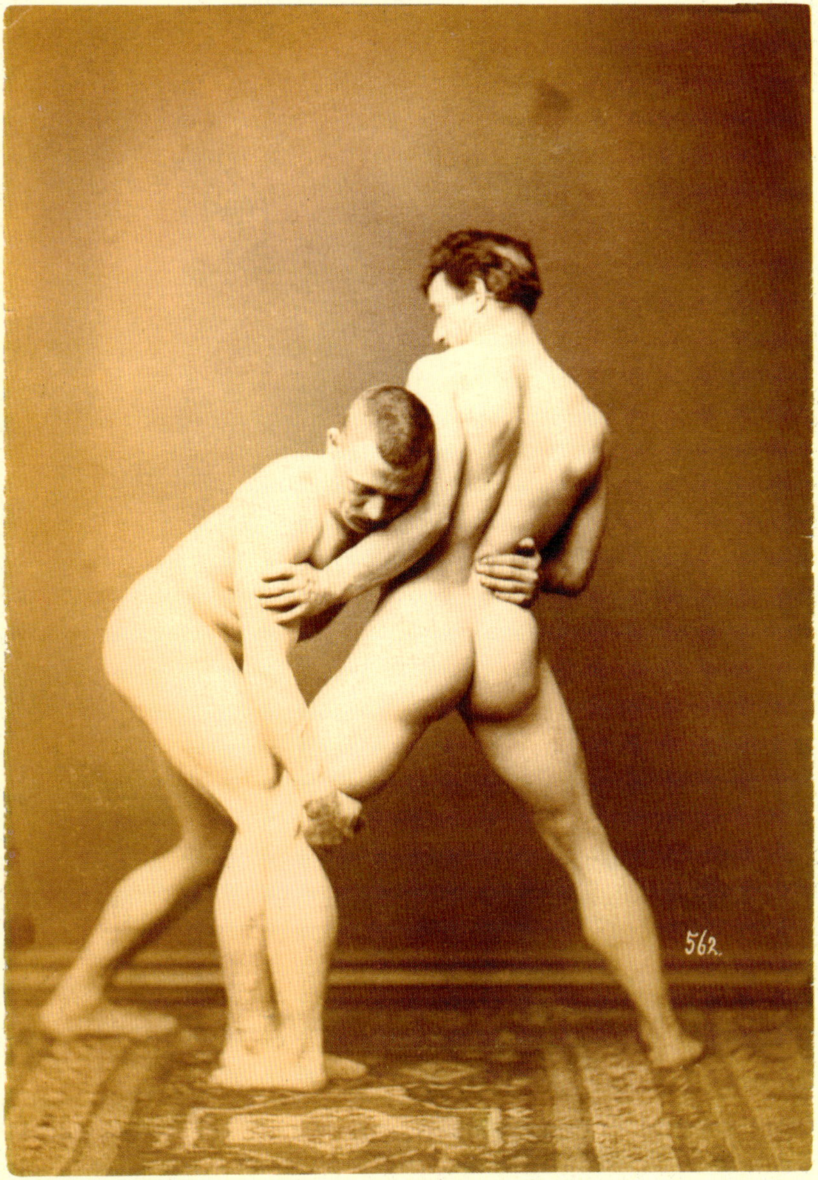

Unidentified wrestlers.
Albumen print, c. 1880.

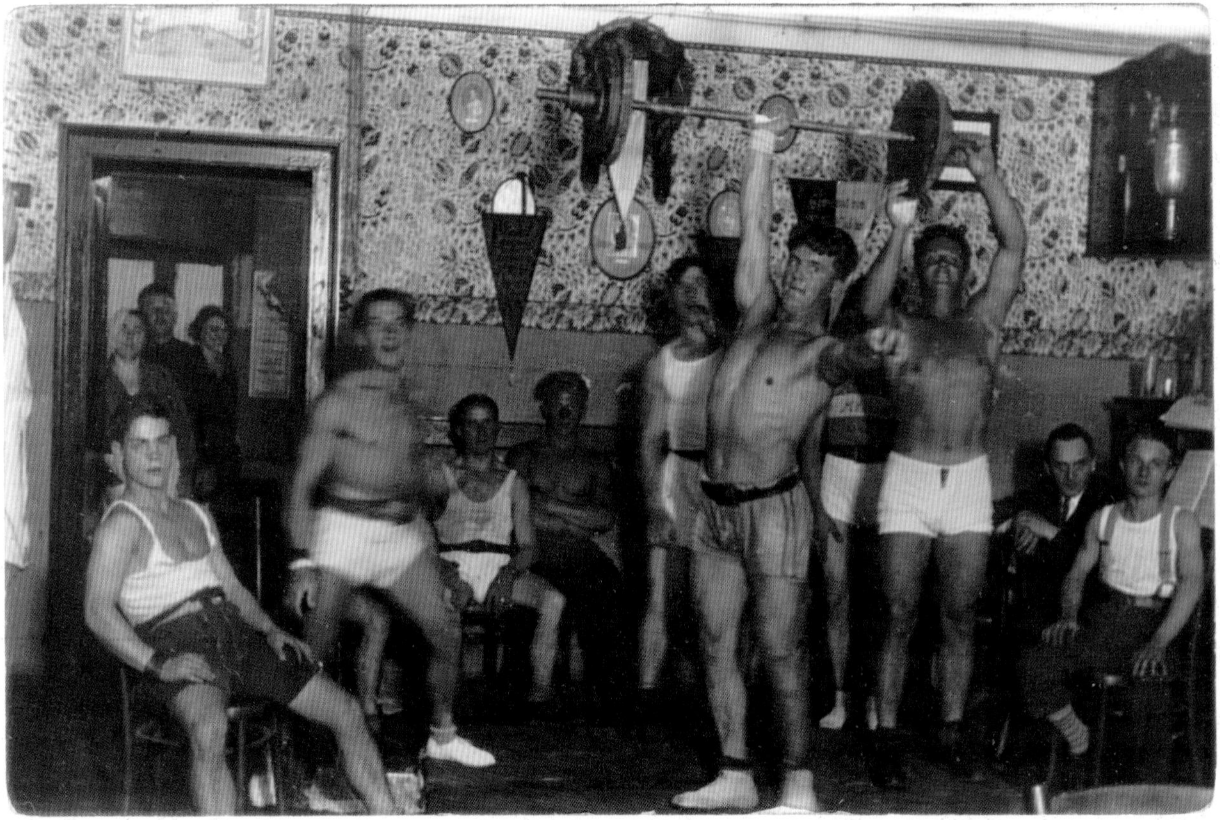

Anonymous German athletes.
Postcard, c. 1920.

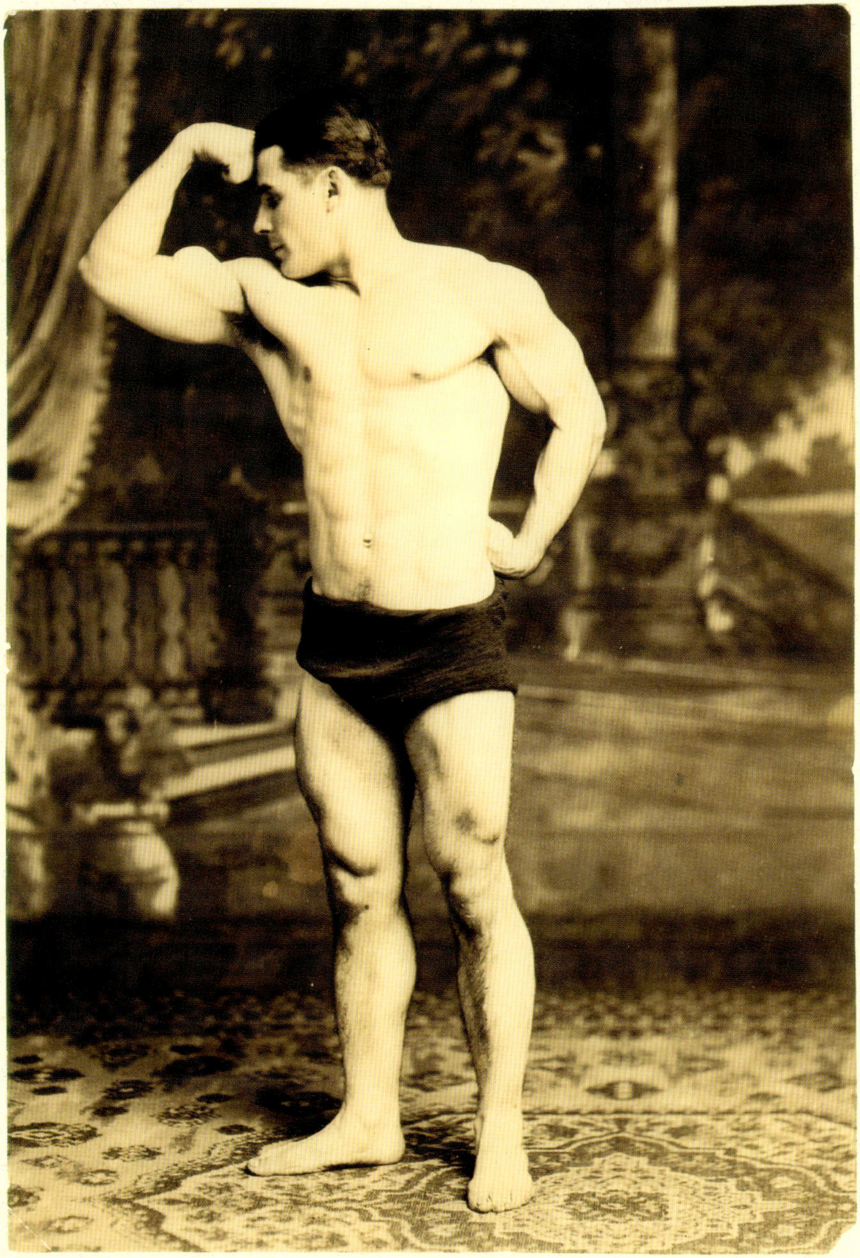

Anonymous studio portrait.
Silverprint, c. 1910.

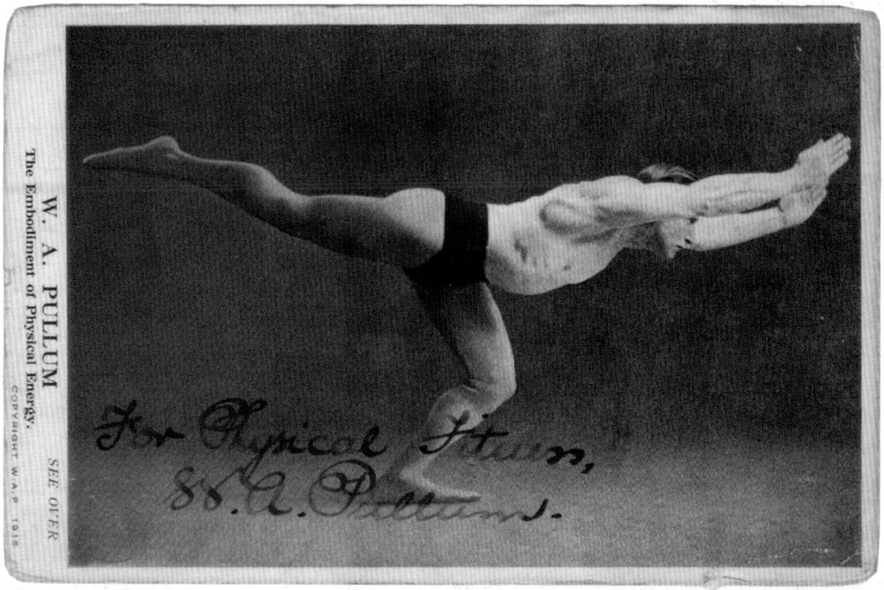

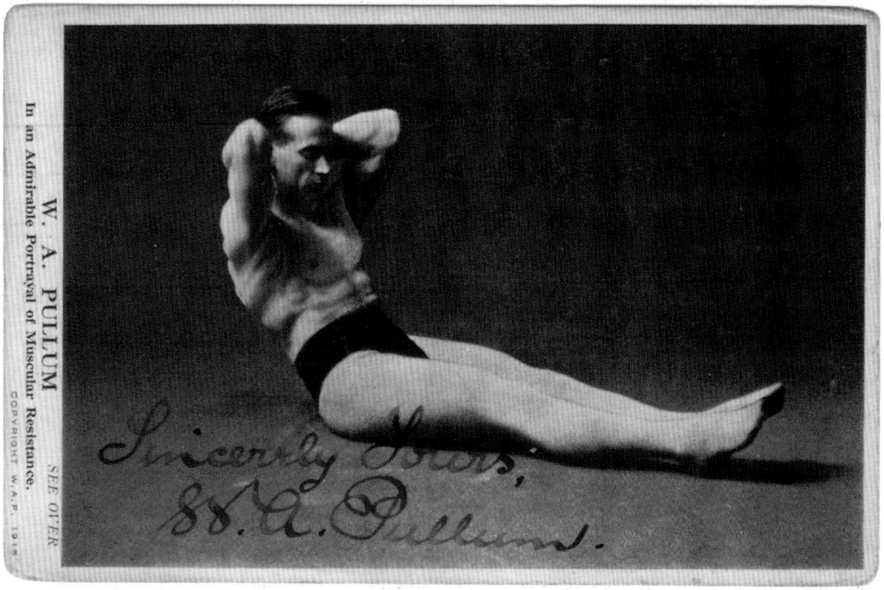

Wm. A. Pullum, strongman and instructor.
British postcards, 1915.

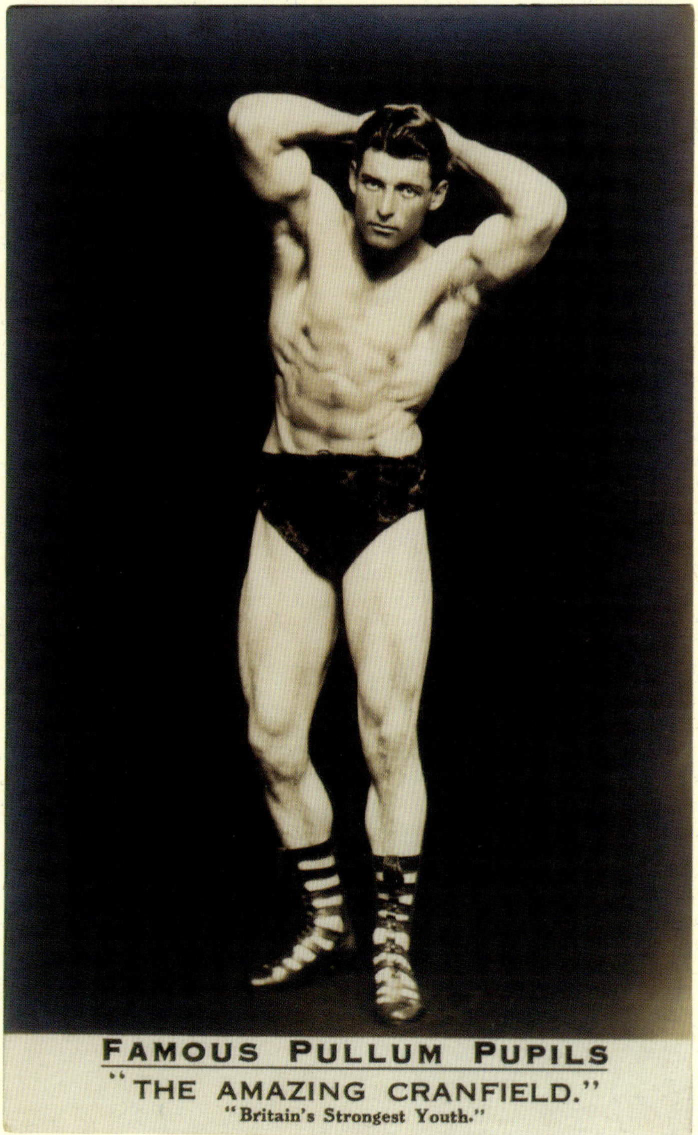

T. W. Cranfield.
One of a series of British postcards promoting Pullum's mail-order bodybuilding course, c. 1920.

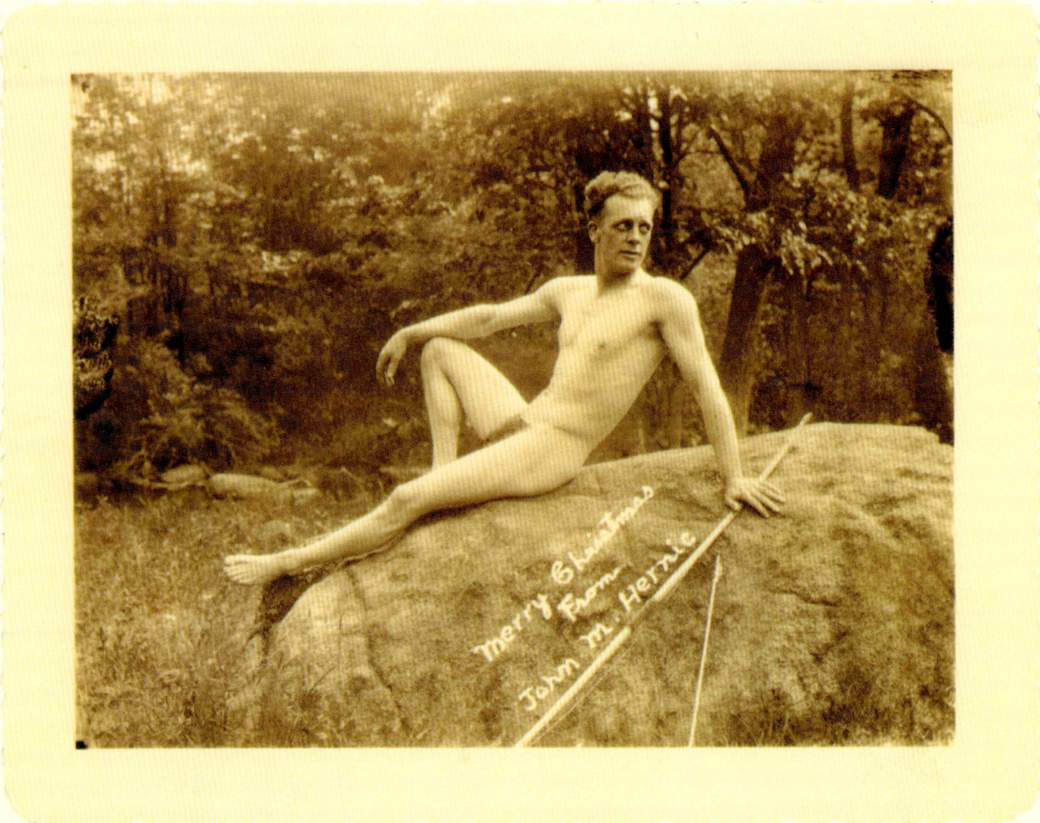

John M. Hernic, photographer, instructor and American mail-order pioneer.
Self-portrait snapshot, c. 1920.

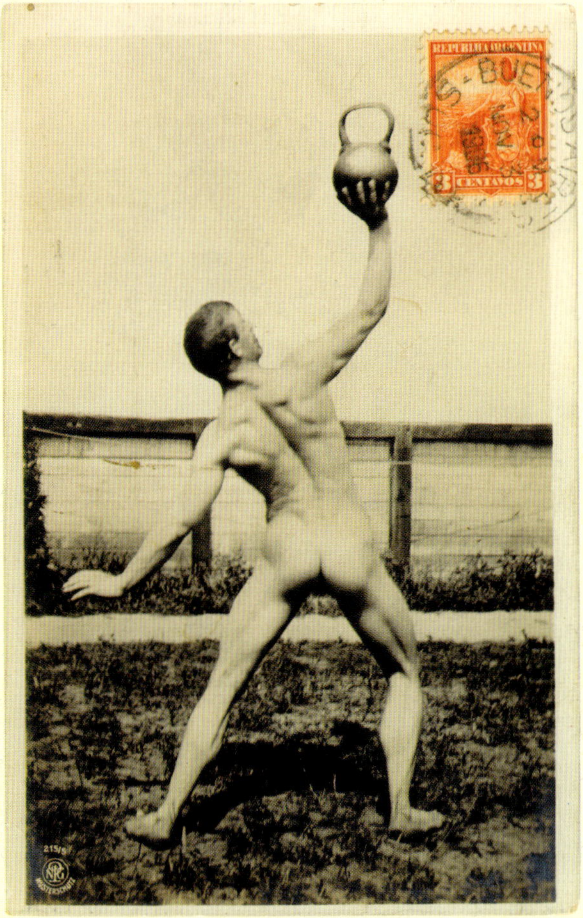

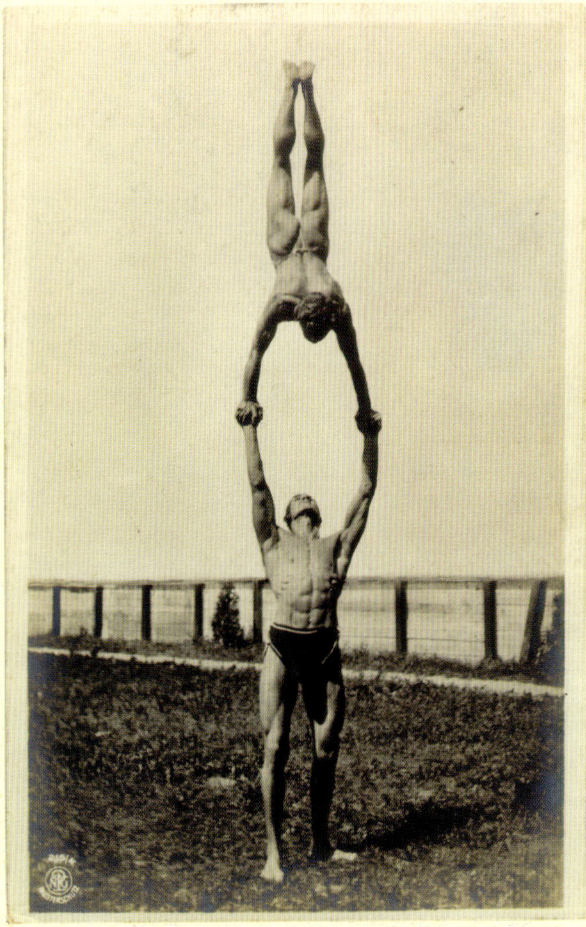

(*Left*) Anonymous German postcard
with Buenos Aires postmark, 1906.
(*Right*) German or Argentine postcard
stamped "NPG Musterschutz," c. 1906.

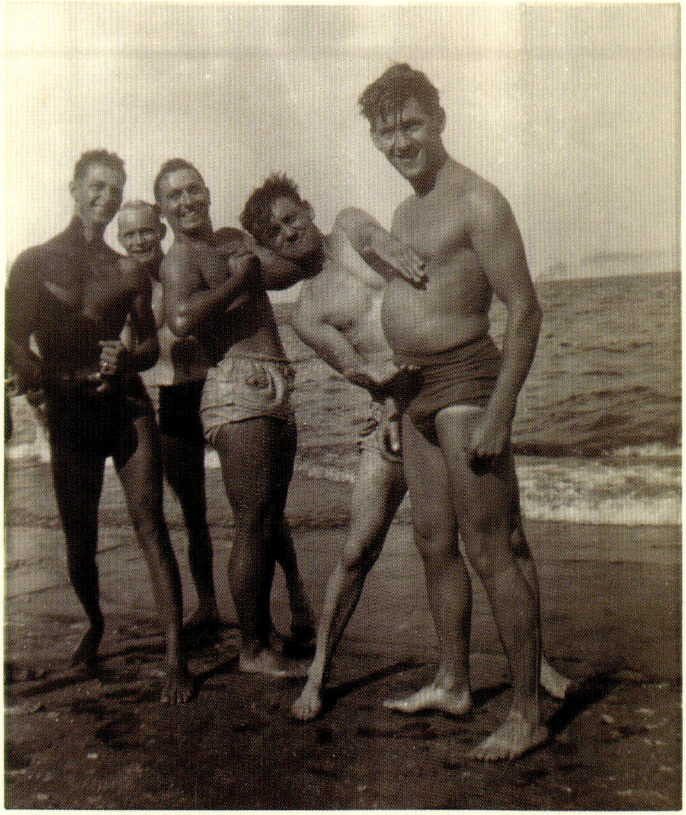

Anonymous snapshot, c. 1940.

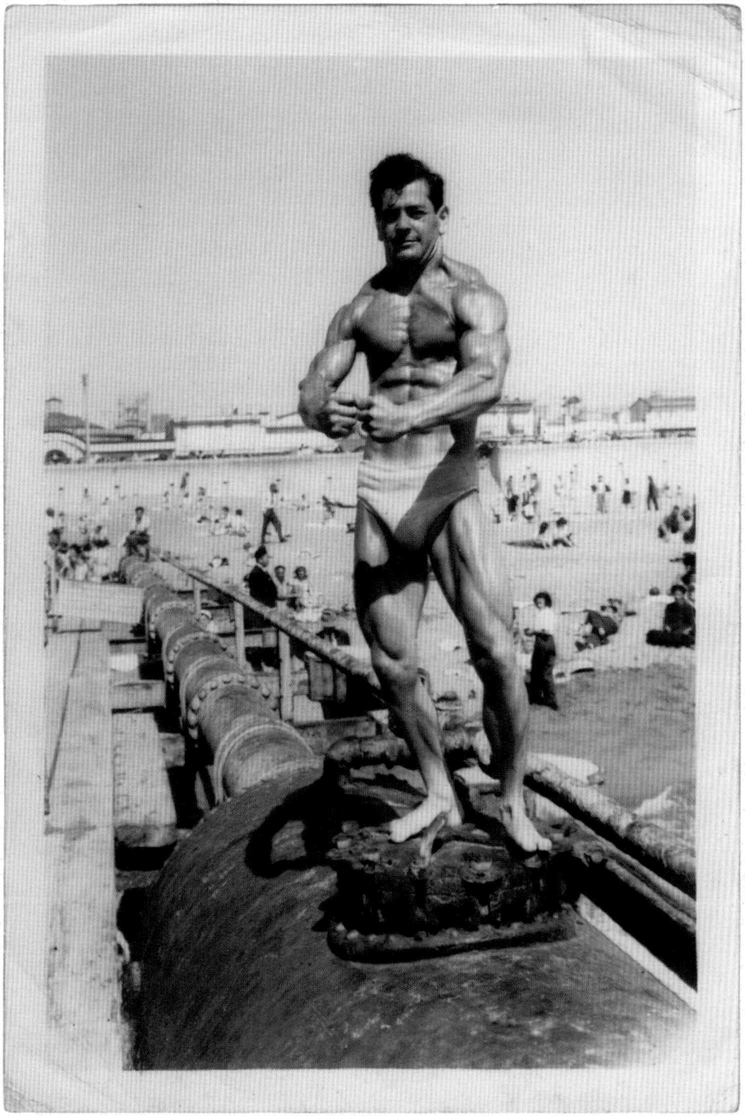

Elias Rodrigues, Mr. California.
Snapshot, c. 1948.

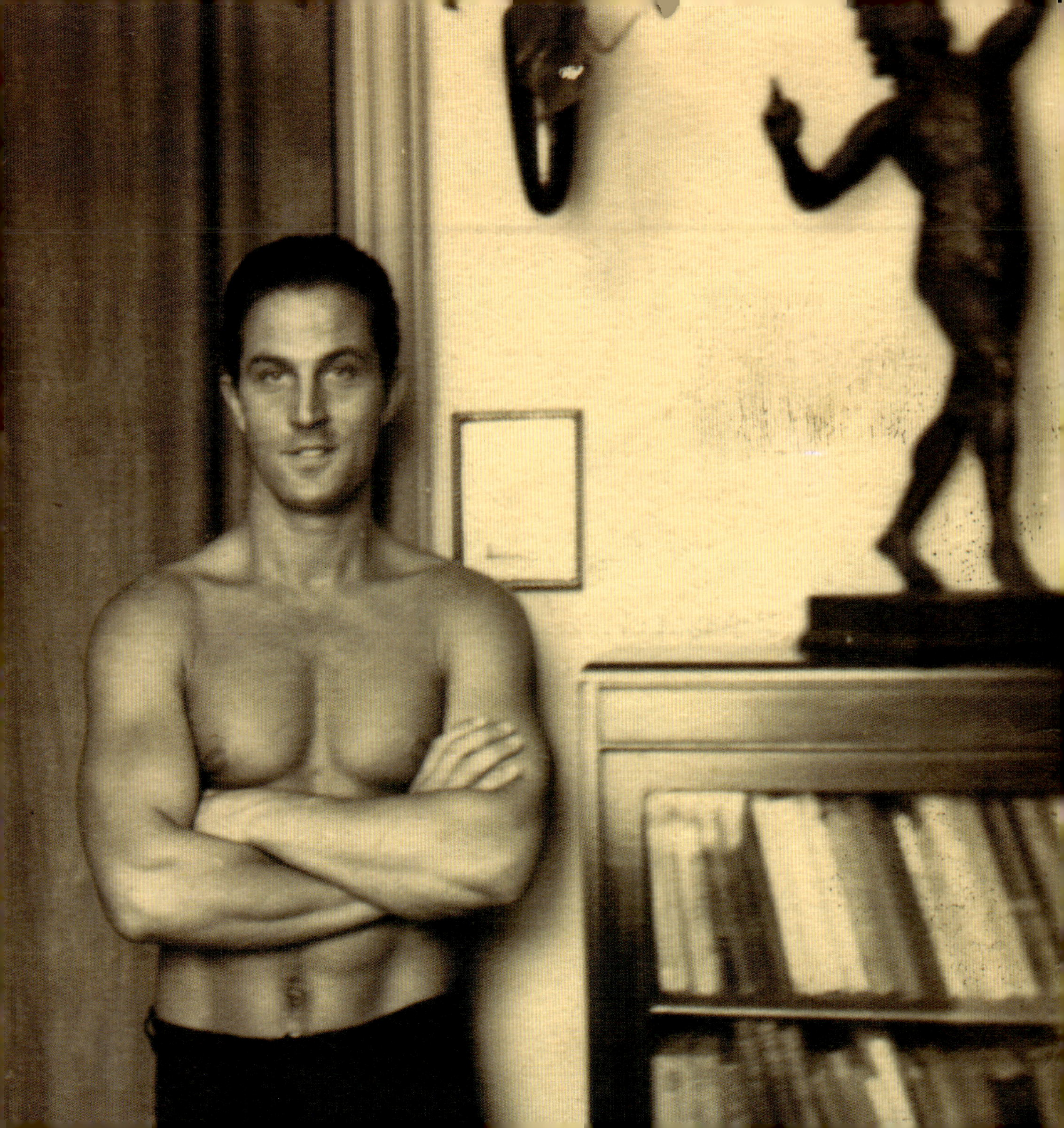

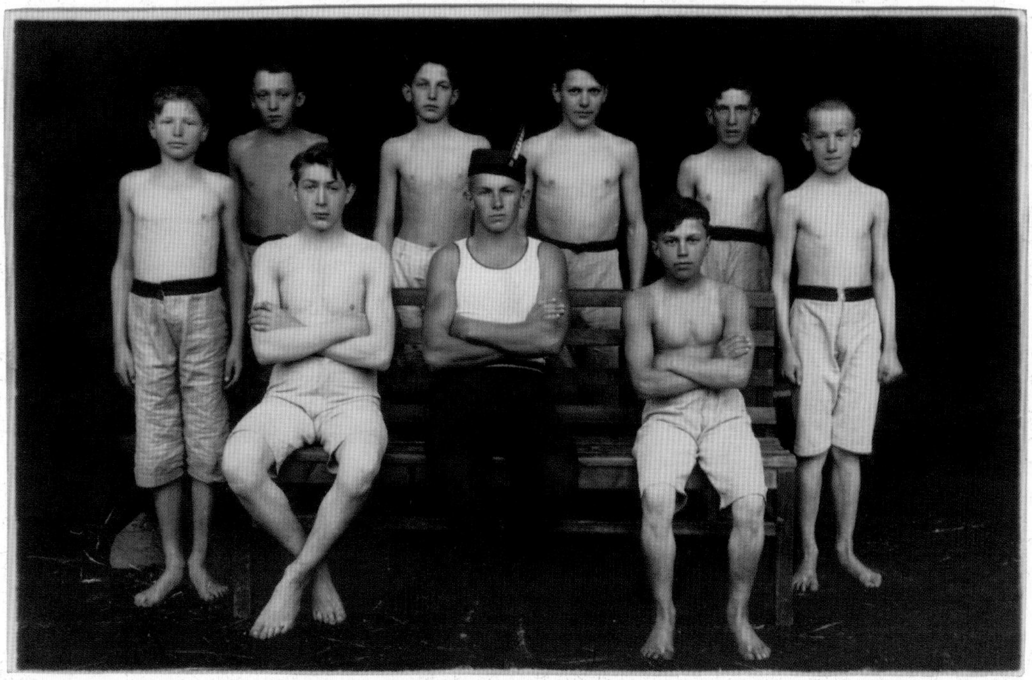

(Opposite) Tony Sansone, famous model and gym owner. Snapshot from the collection of Lon Hanagan, c. 1930. *(Above)* Anonymous Czech athletes. Postcard, 1926.

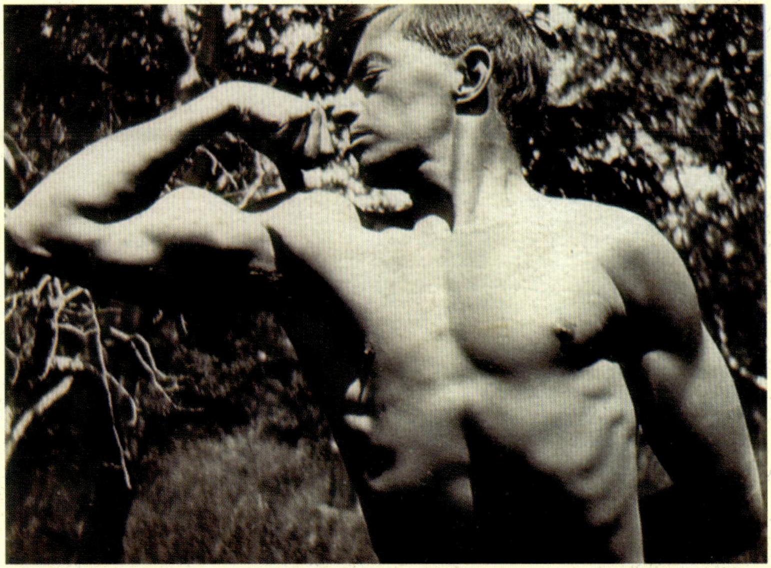
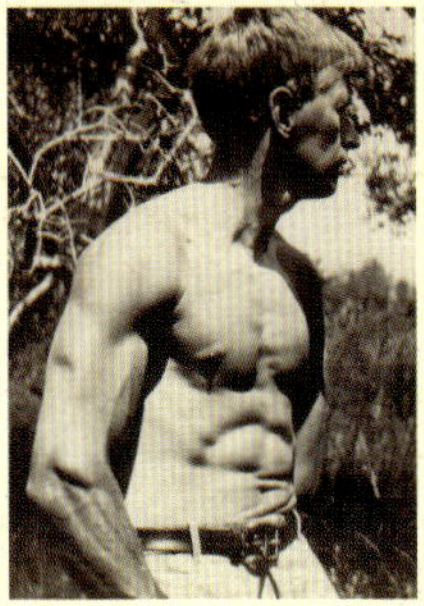
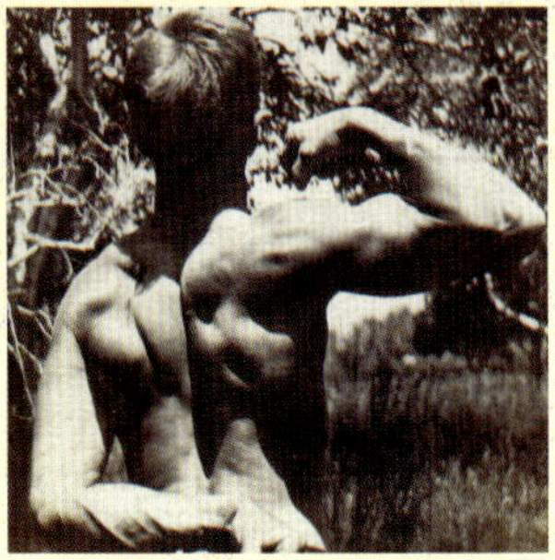
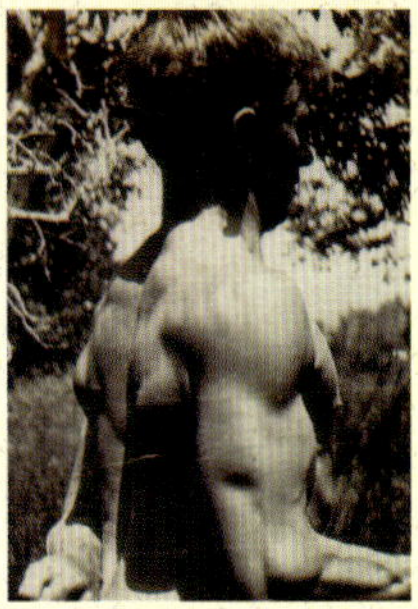

Anonymous snapshots,
c. 1940.

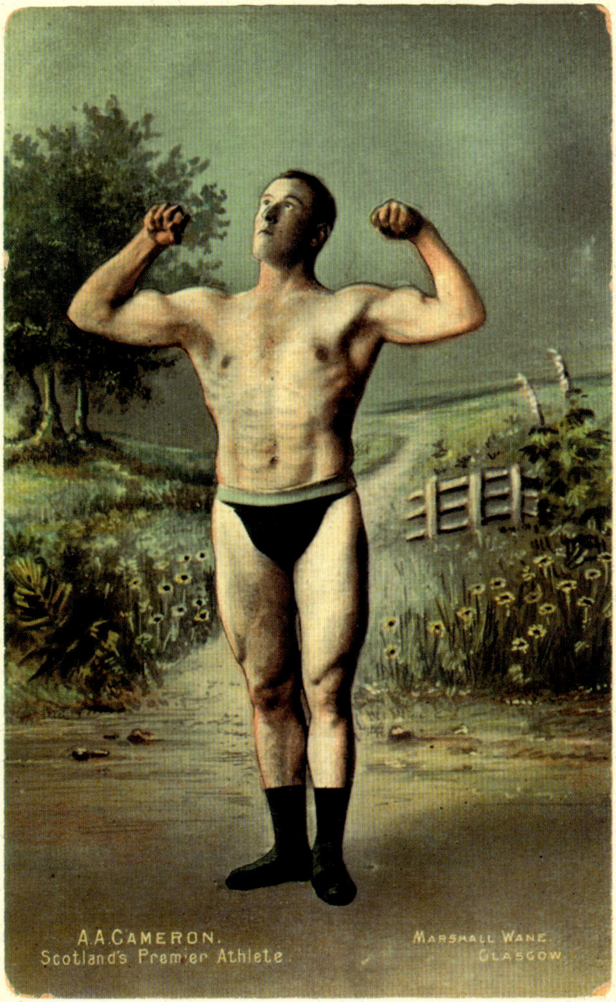

A. A. Cameron, Scotland's Premier Athlete, by Wane.
Color postcard, c. 1915.

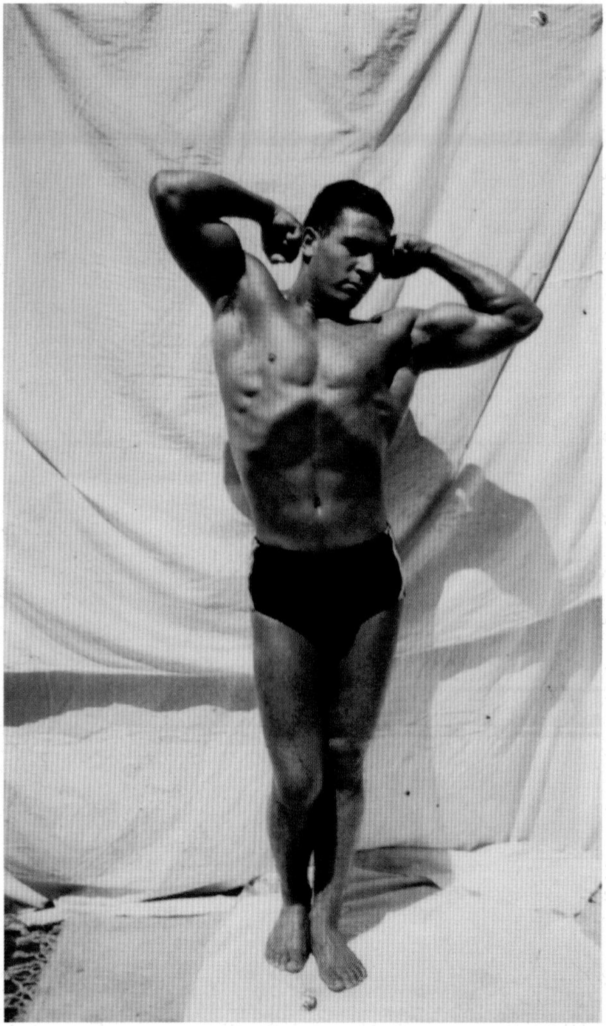

Jack LaLanne, American television personality, Berkeley, Calif. Snapshot, c.1940.

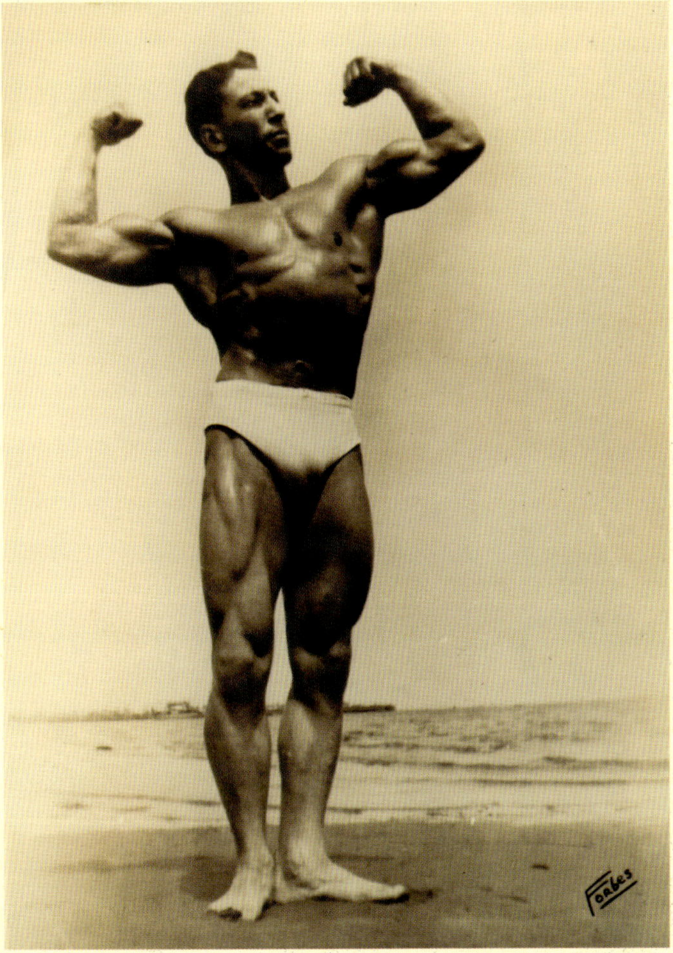

Dan Lurie, publisher of Muscle Training Illustrated *magazine* by Earl Forbes. Silverprint, c. 1940.

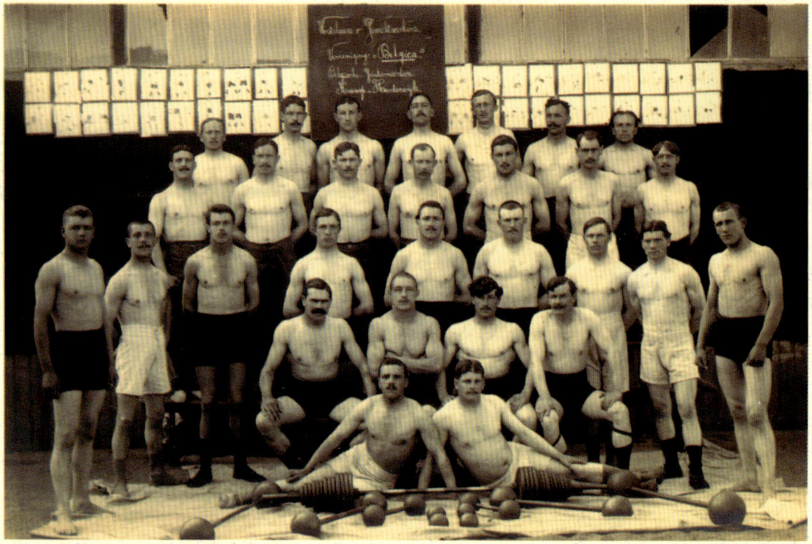

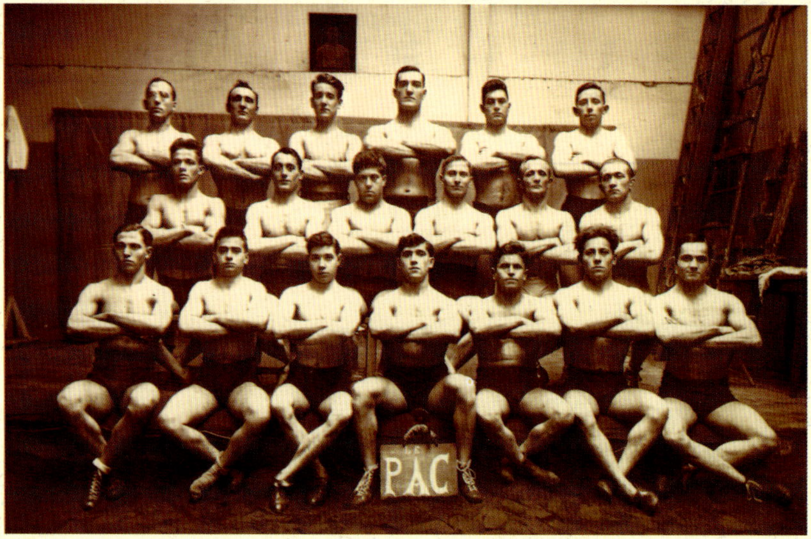

(Top) Belgian athletic team. Unattributed postcard, c. 1920.
(Bottom) French Athletic Team by Ch. Paul DuFresne.
Silverprint, c. 1925.
(Opposite) Folsom (Calif.) State Prison Games.
Silverprint, 1913.

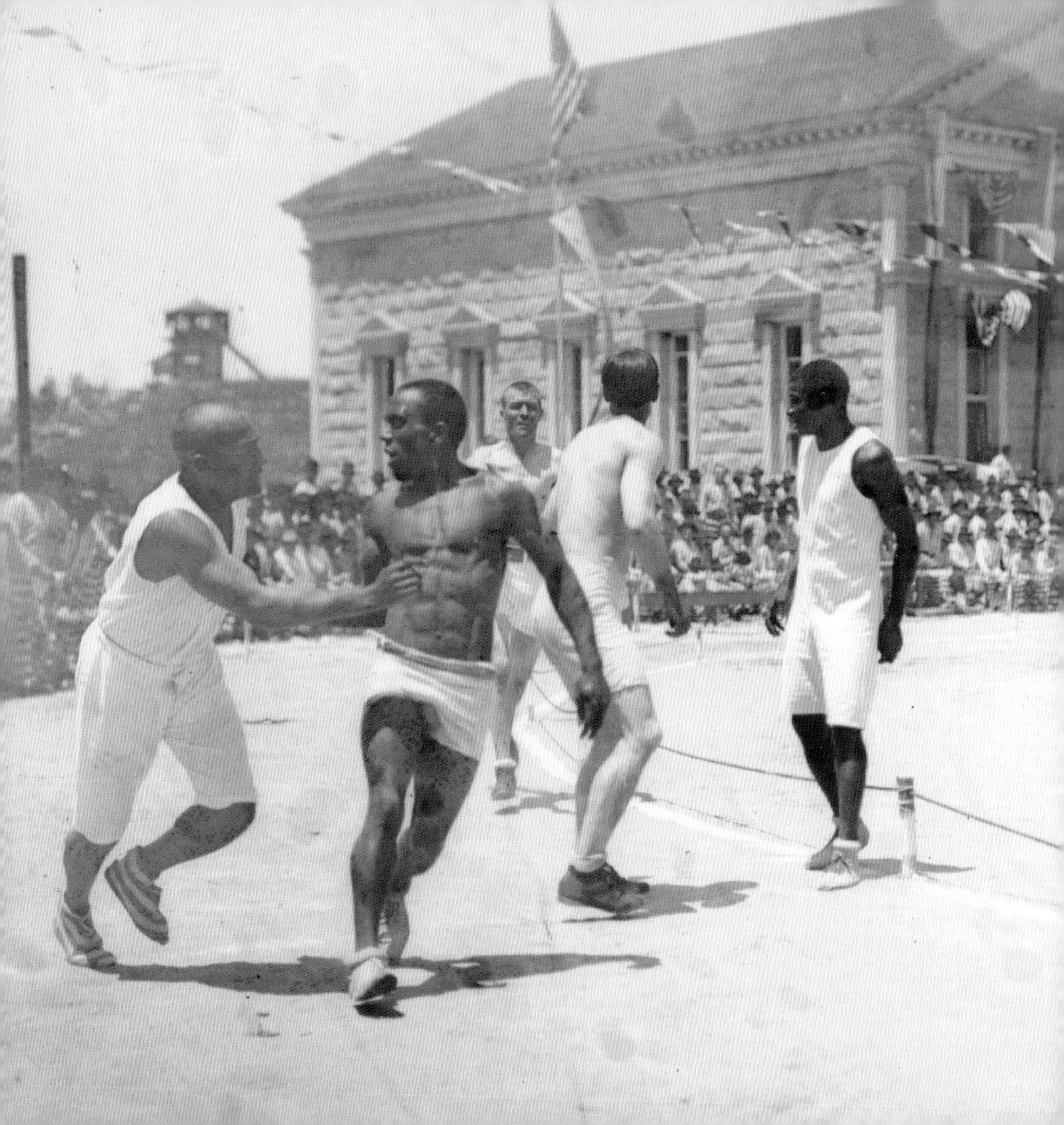

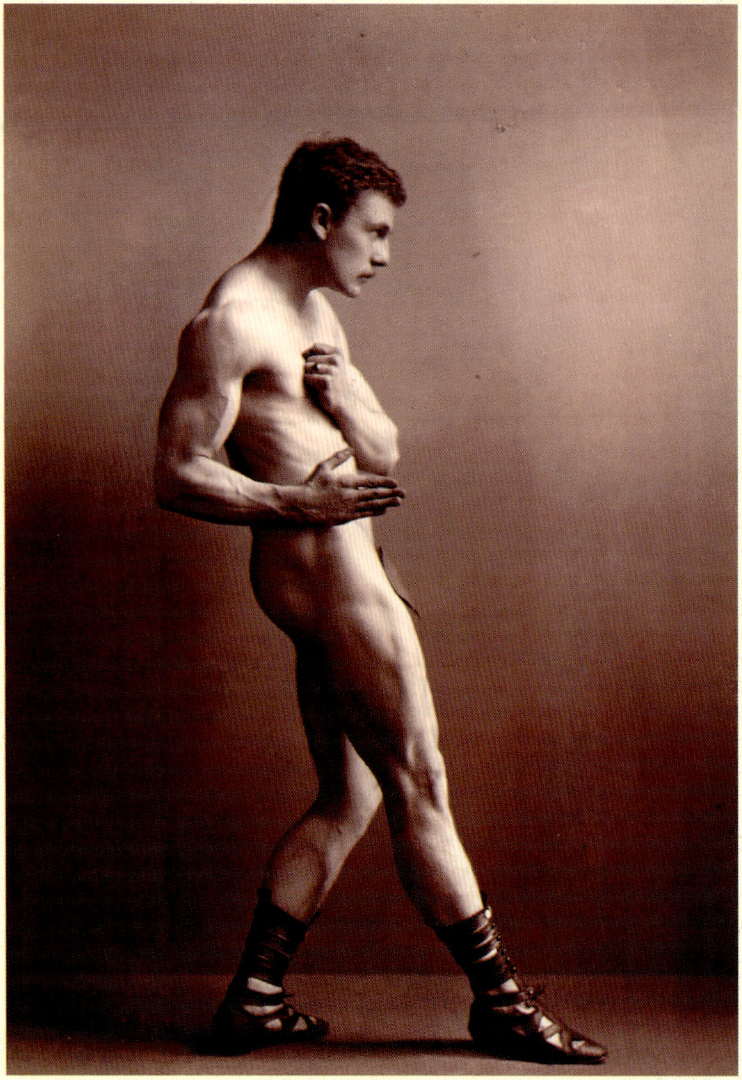

Max Milian, German strongman and juggler in a pose plastique.
Unattributed cabinet card, c. 1900.

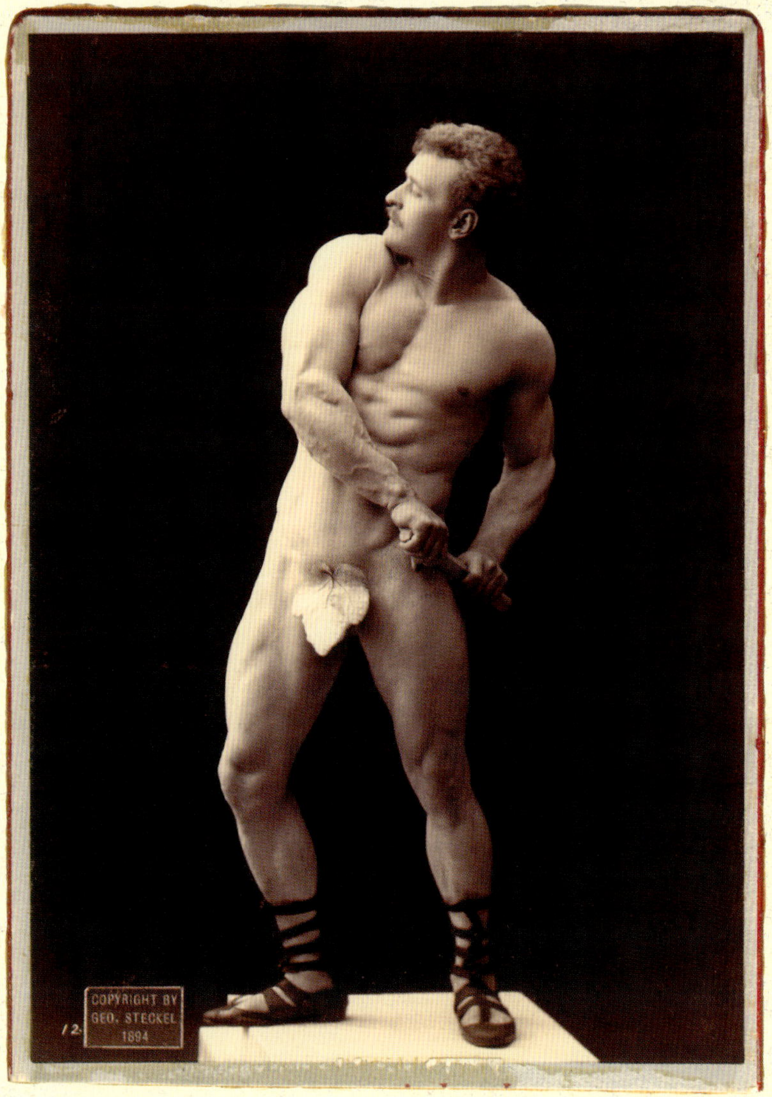

Eugen Sandow (Friedrich Muller),
famous Prussian strongman by Geo. Steckel.
Cabinet card, 1894.

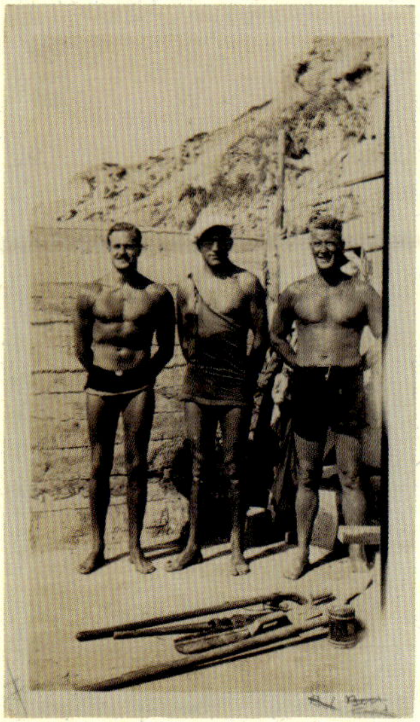

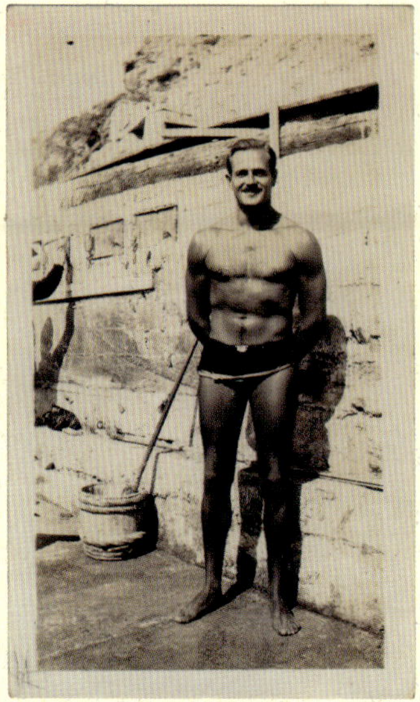

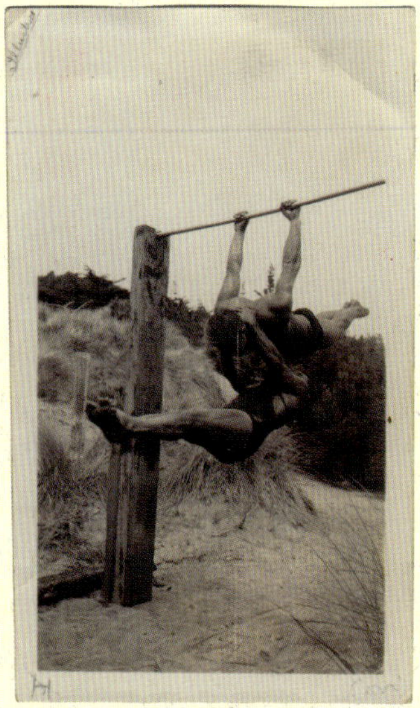

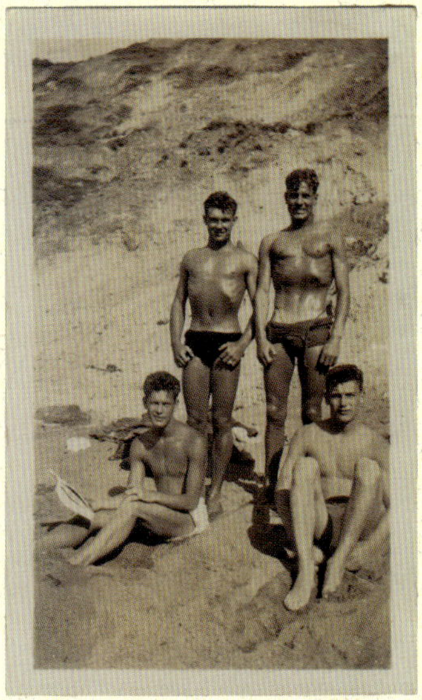

(This and opposite page)
"Cliff, Elbert, Bill, Glenn, Ed, Conrad and Fred."
California snapshots, c. 1925.

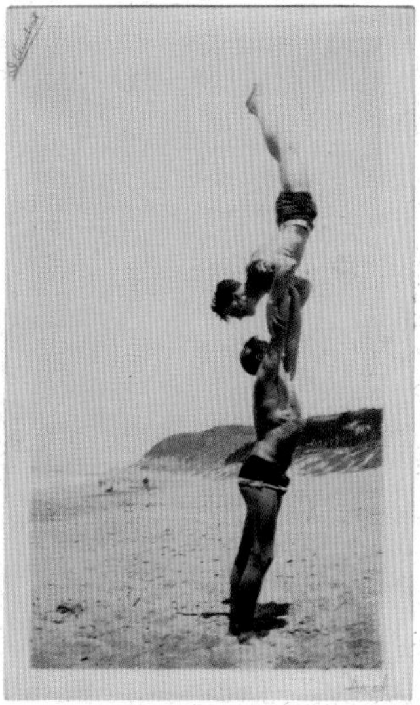
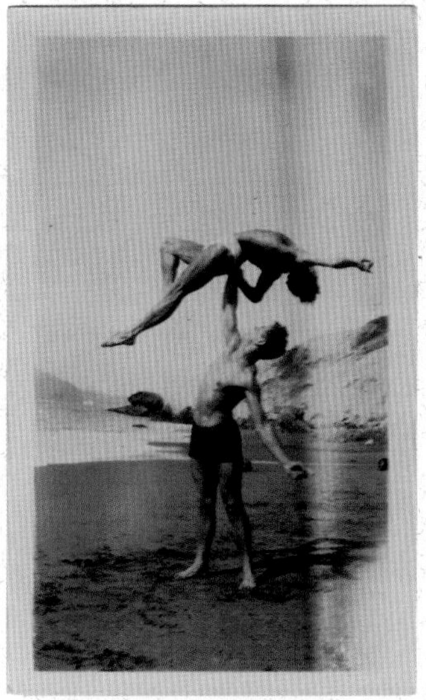
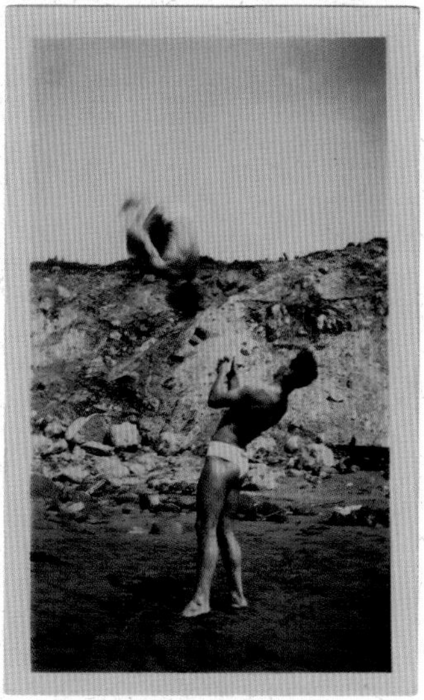
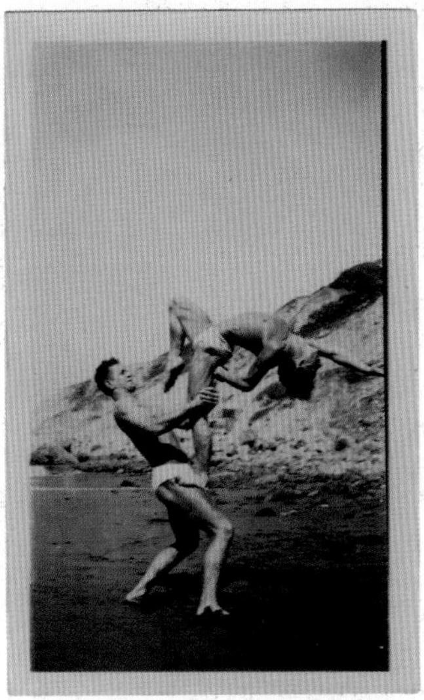

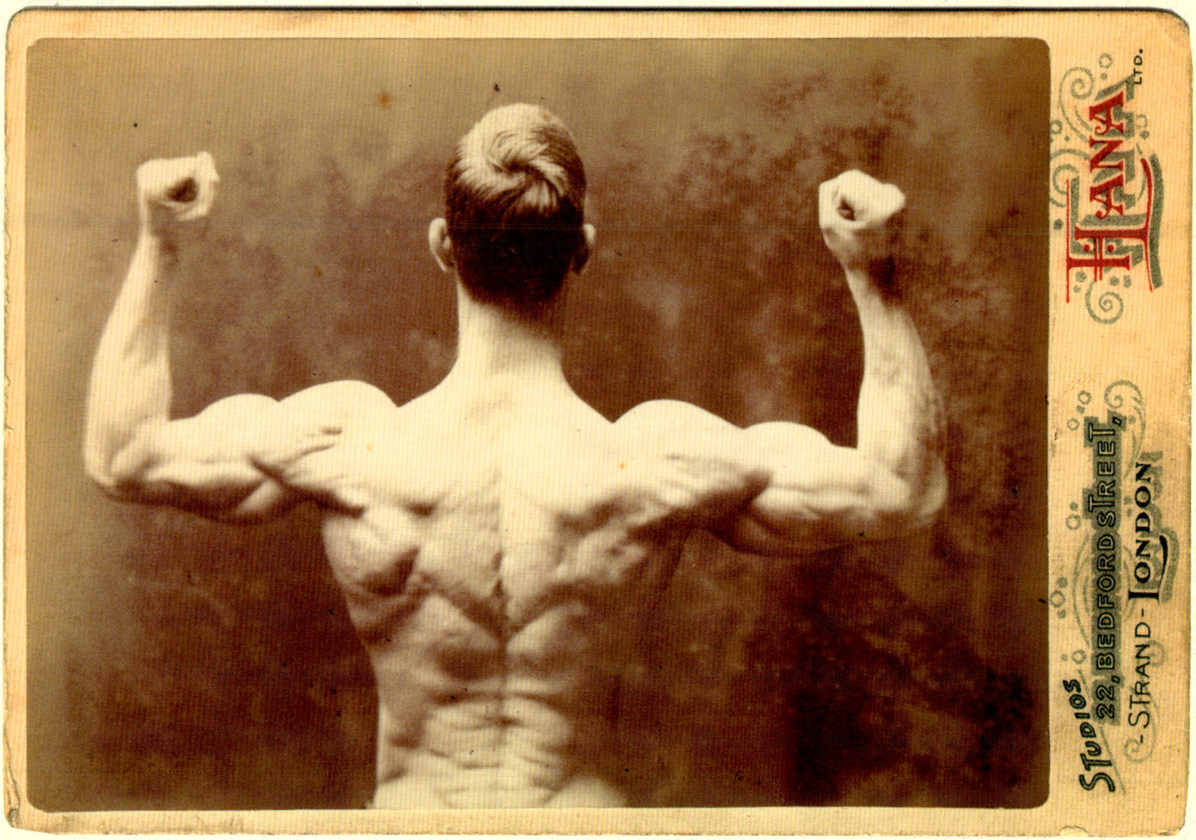

Charles Vansittart, Yukon gold prospector
by Hana, London.
Cabinet card, c. 1890.

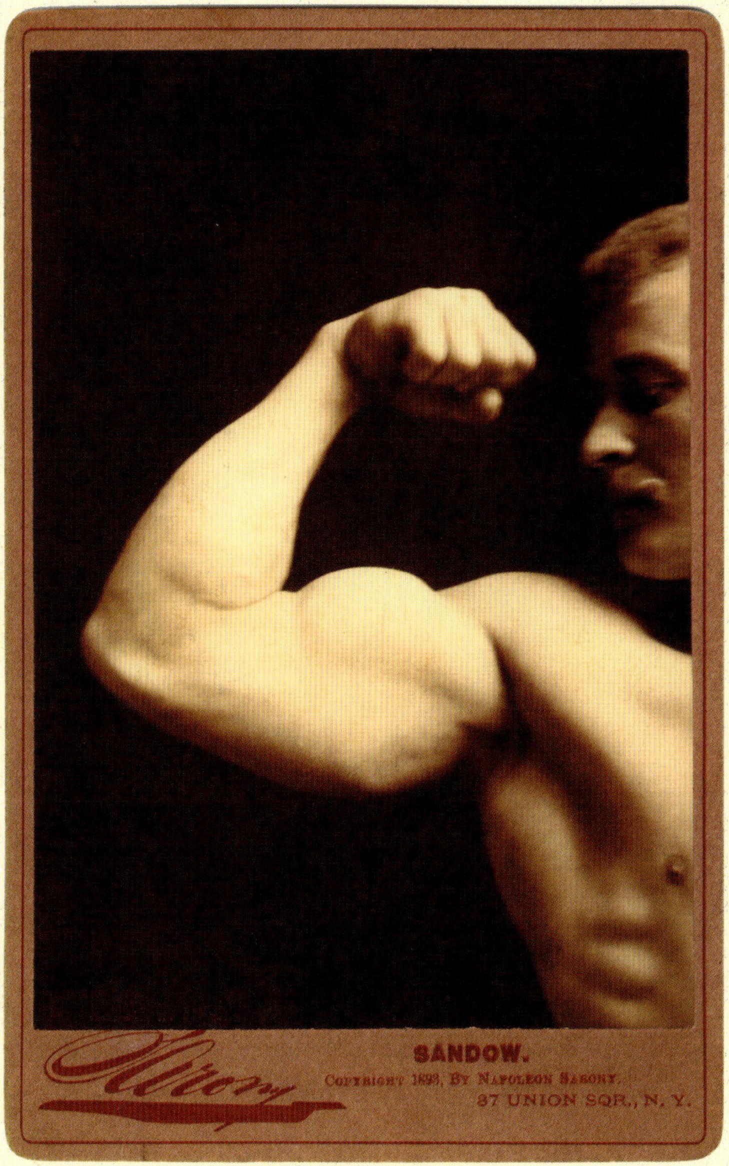

Eugen Sandow by Sarony,
New York City. Cabinet card, 1896.

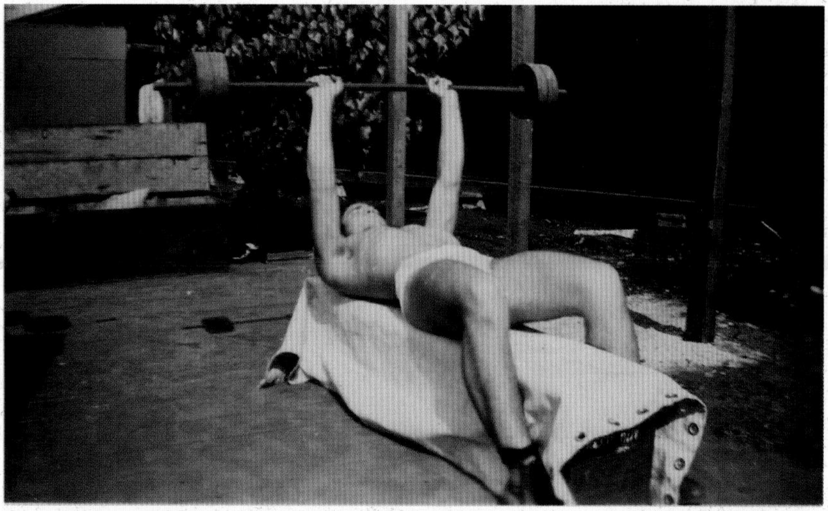

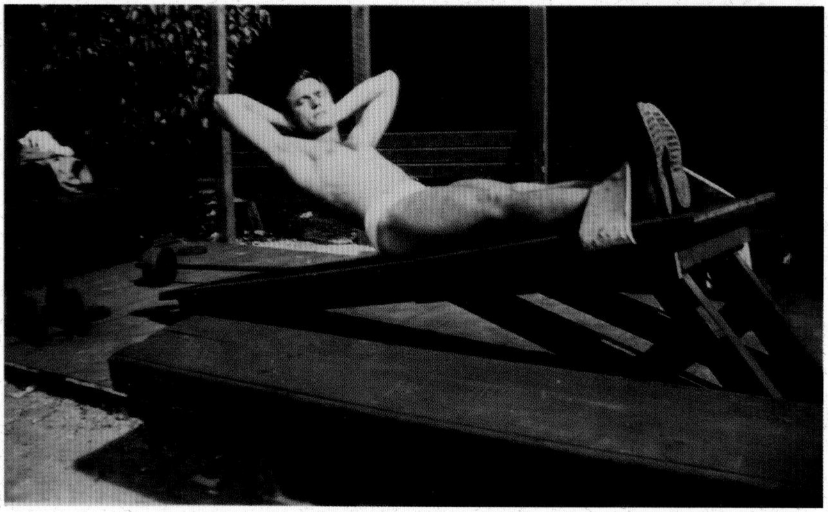

(This and opposite page) Anonymous American snapshots, c. 1940.

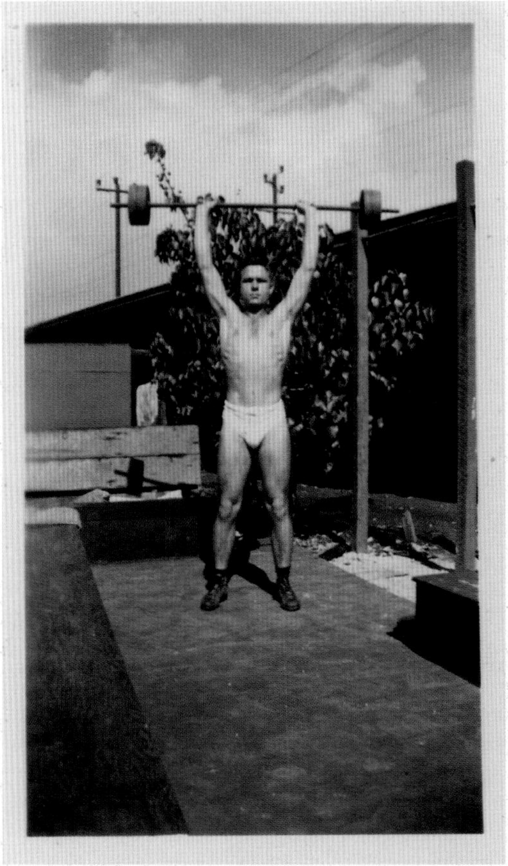

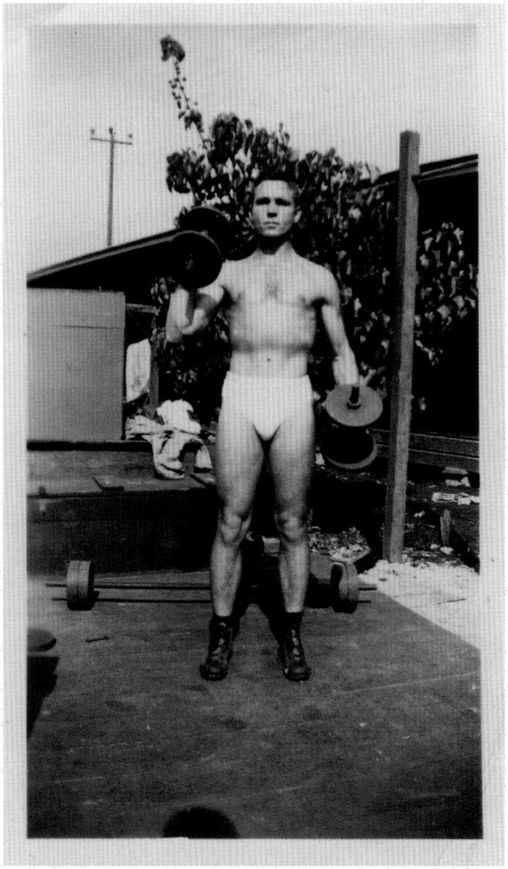

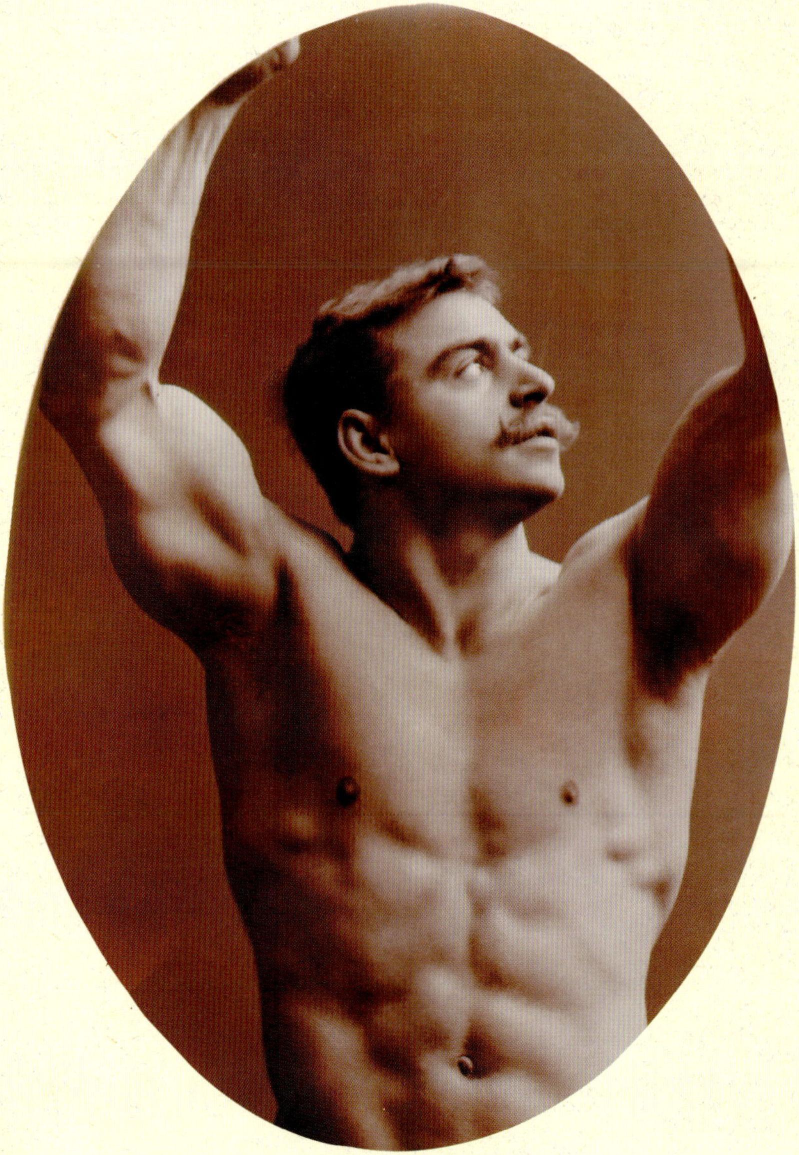

Milo Brinn (Luigi Borra),
Italian wrestler and strongman.
Unattributed cabinet card, c. 1895.

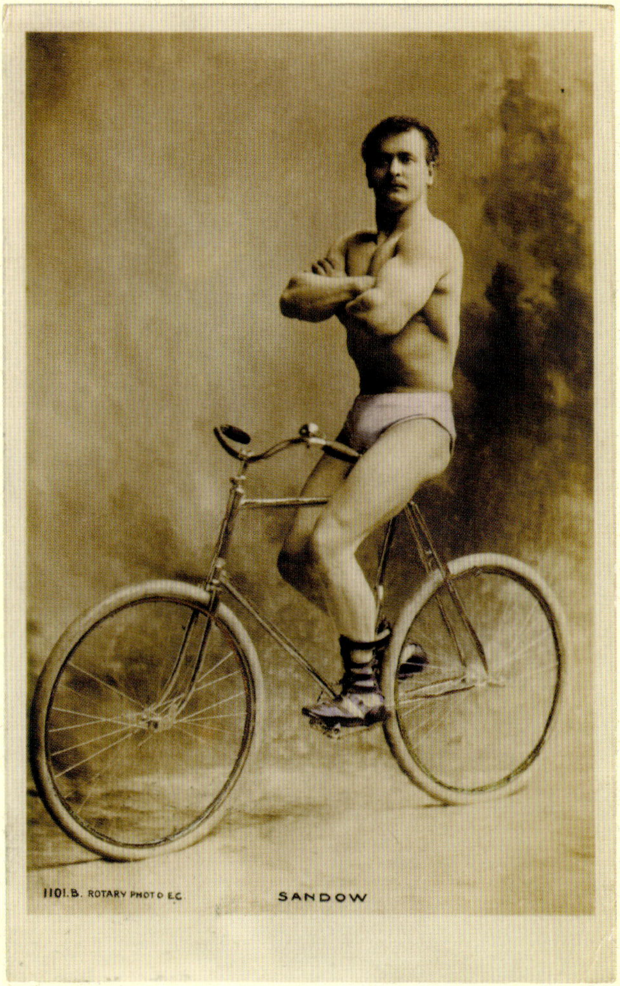

Eugen Sandow, by B. J. Falk.
British postcard, 1896.

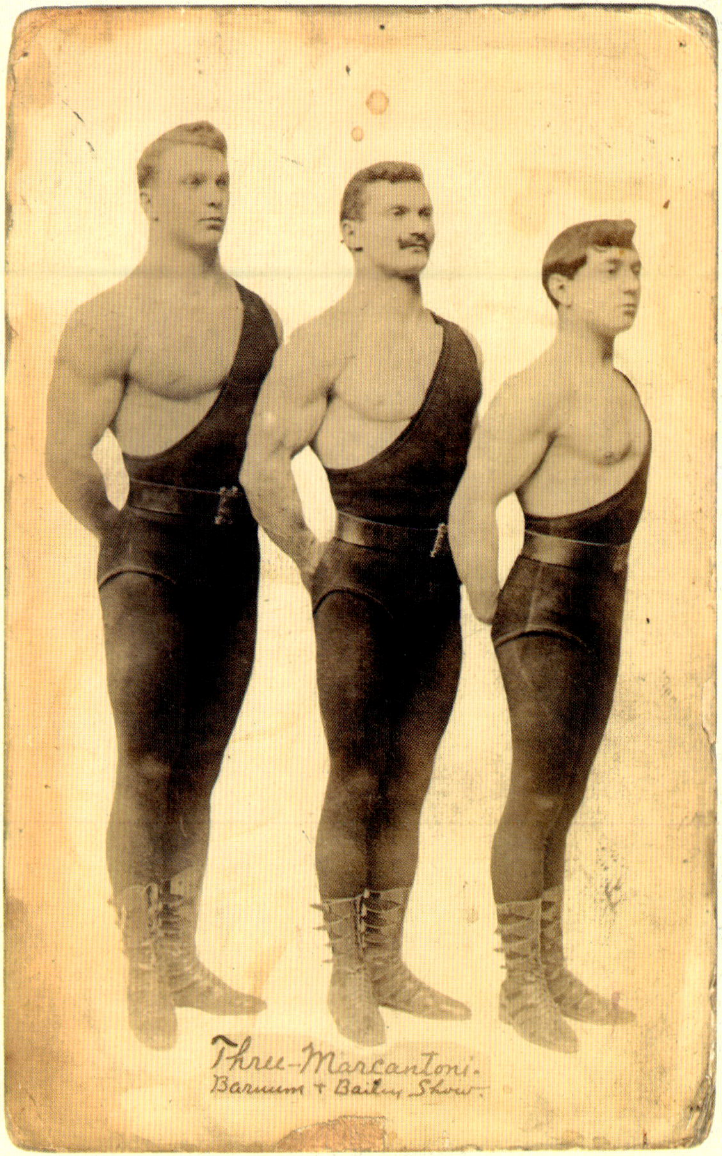

Three Marcantoni, Barnum & Bailey Show.
Postcard, c. 1910.

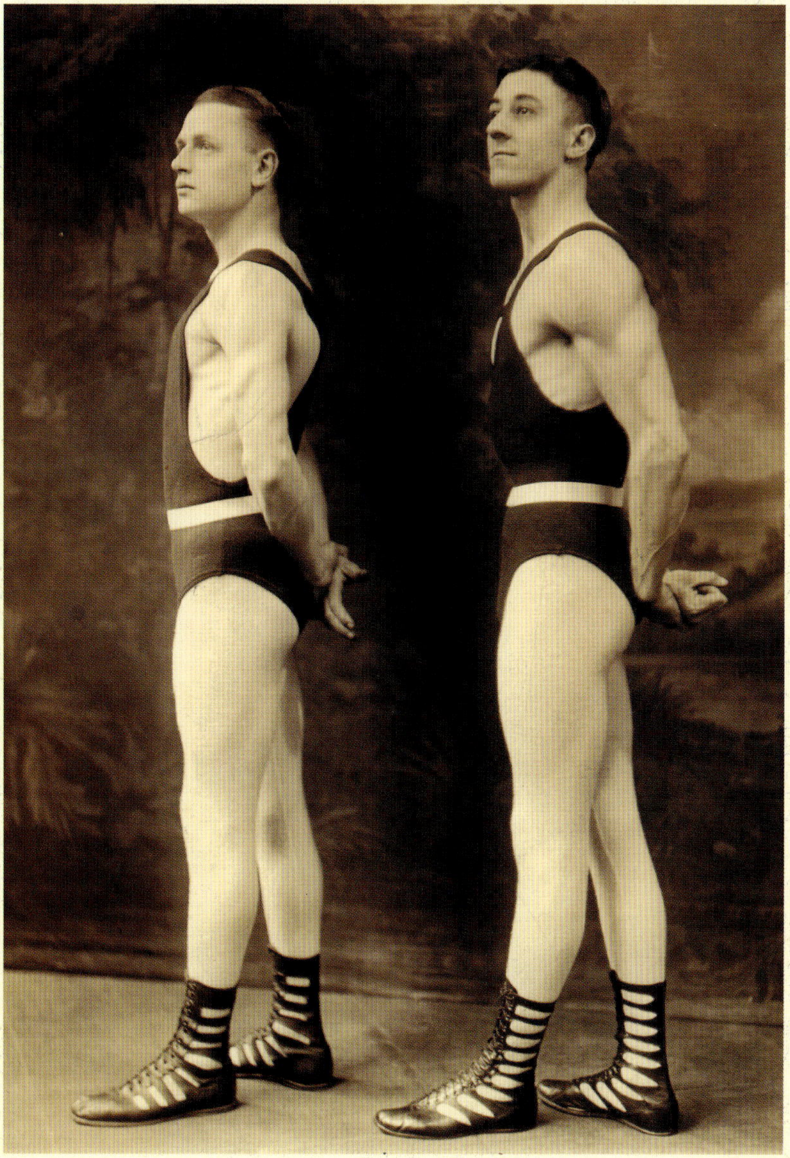

Vaudevillians (?) Mang & Hollatz
by S. E. Stodoford, Pittsburgh, Pa.
Silverprint, 1932.

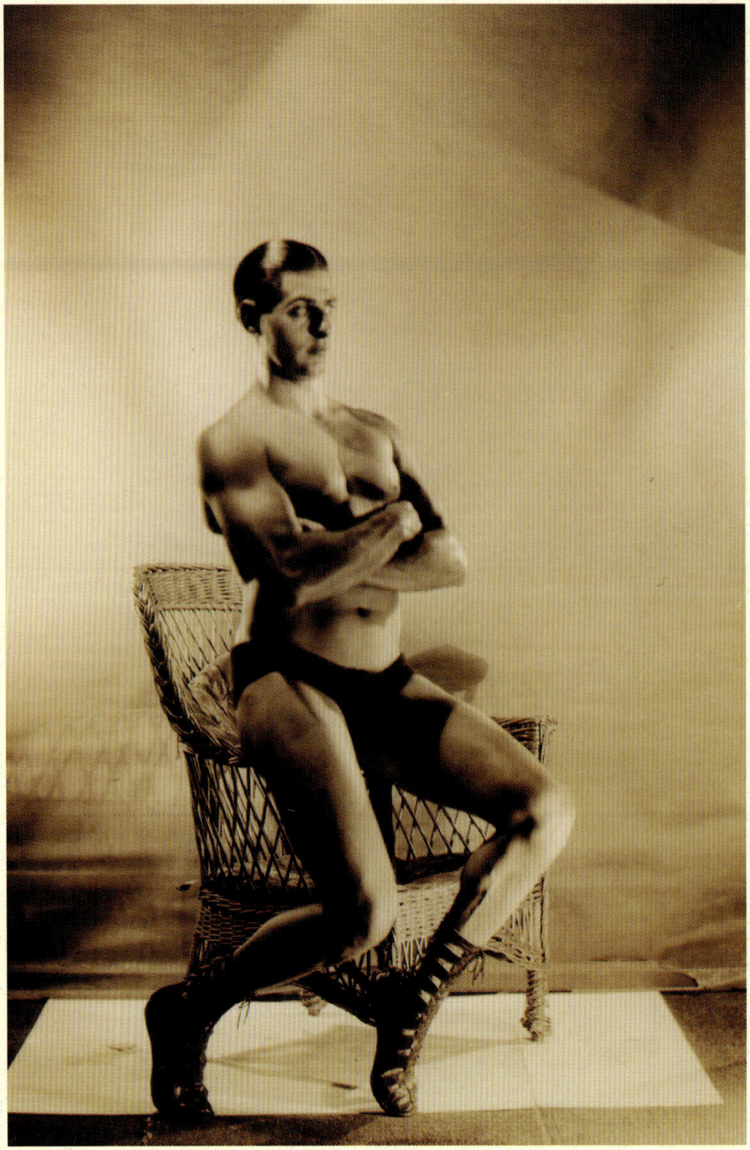

(Above) Milton M. Cohen
by Edwin F. Townsend. Silverprint, c. 1925.
(Opposite) Charlie and his teammates.
Unattributed cyanotype, c. 1900.

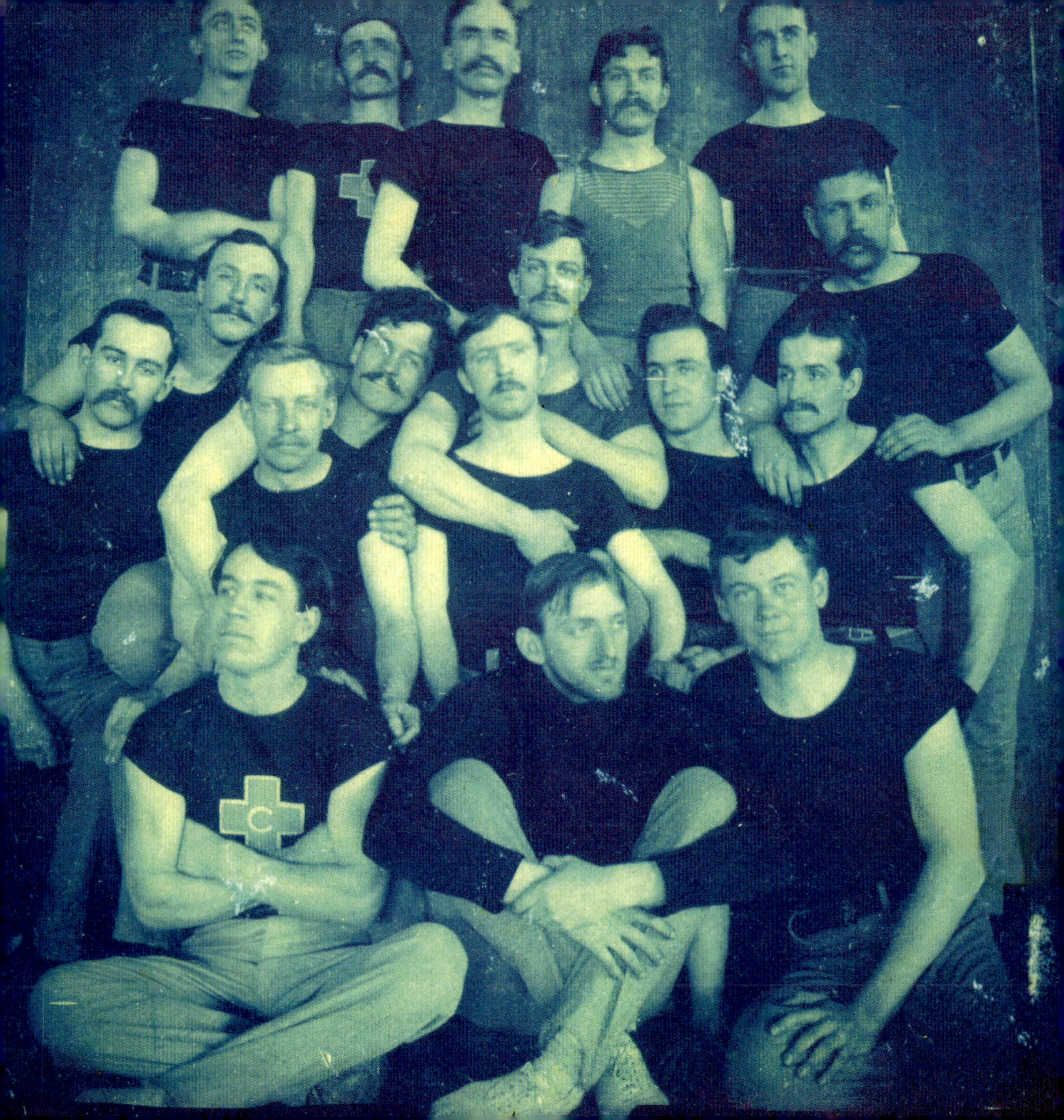

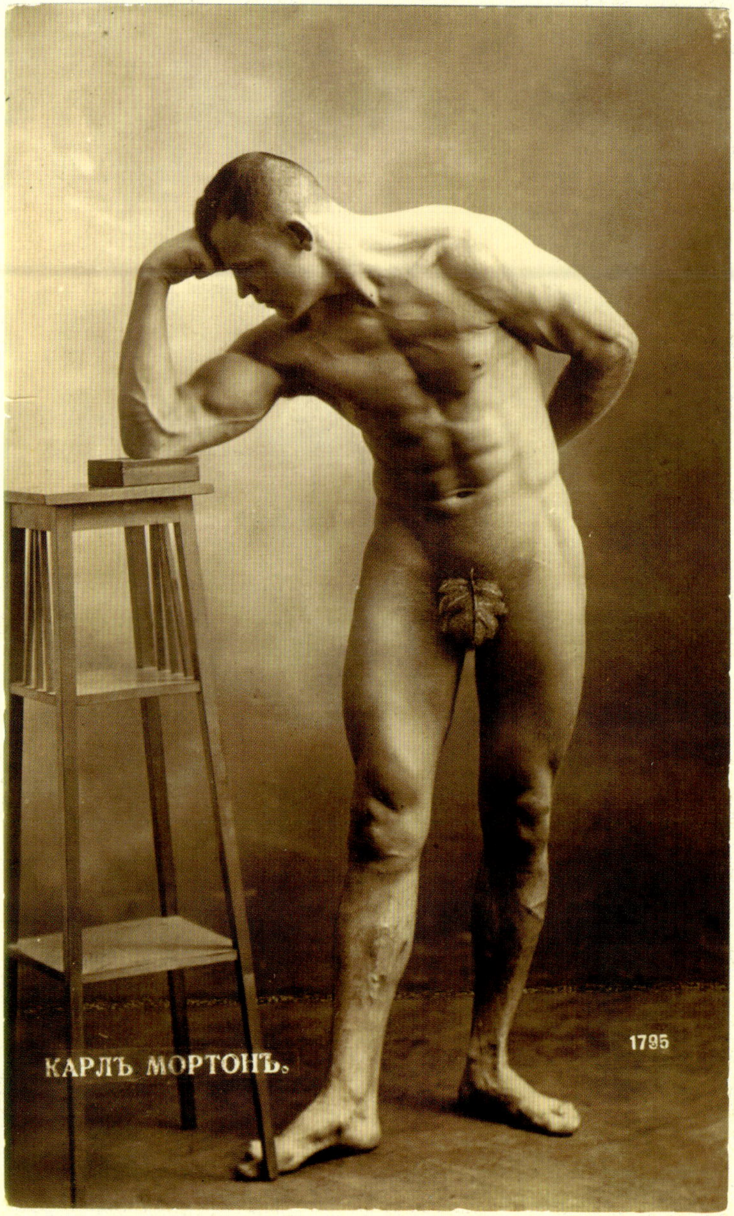

Karl Morton by A. E. Zhenter.
Russian postcard, c. 1915.

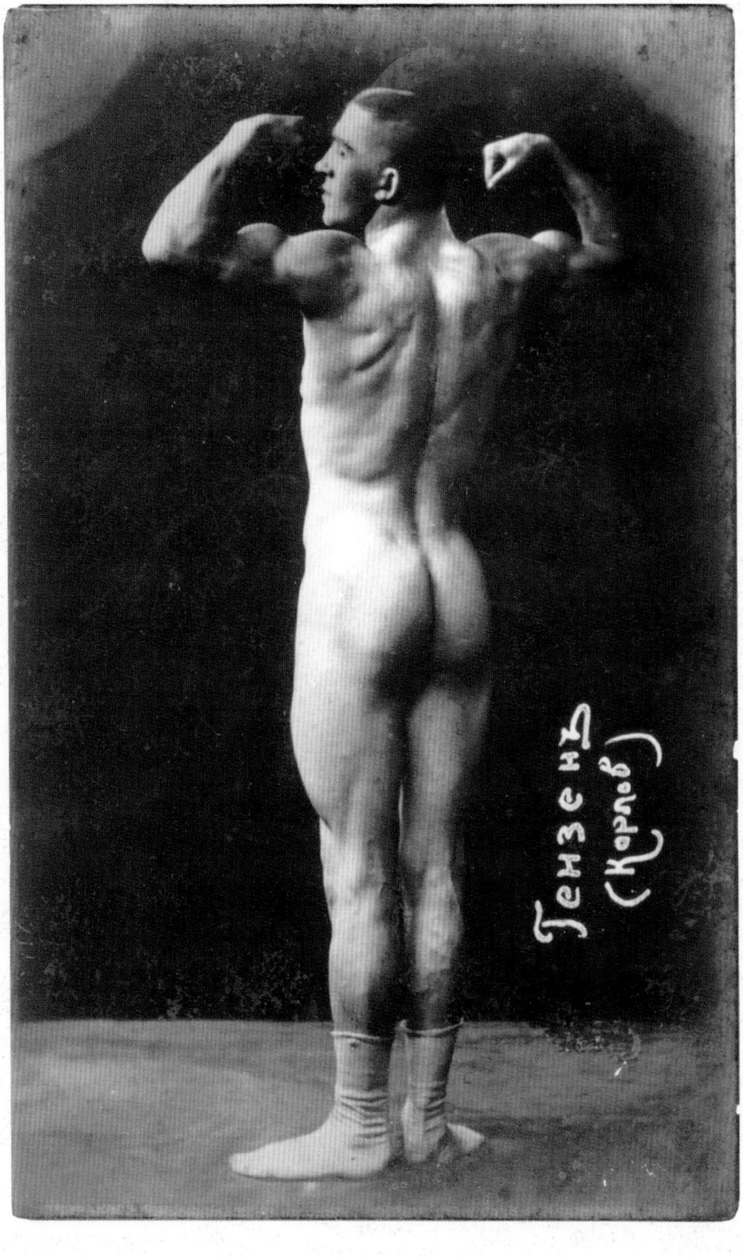

Jenzen (Korlov).
Russian postcard, c. 1915.

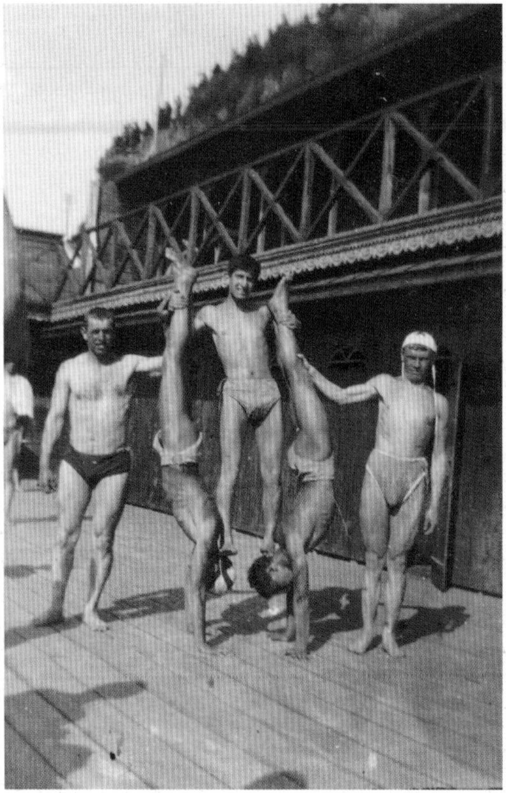

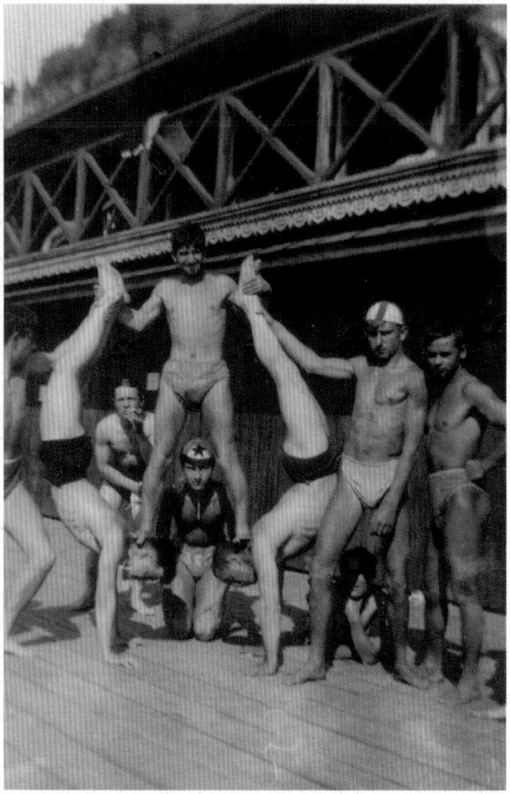

Anonymous Russian snapshots,
c. 1920.

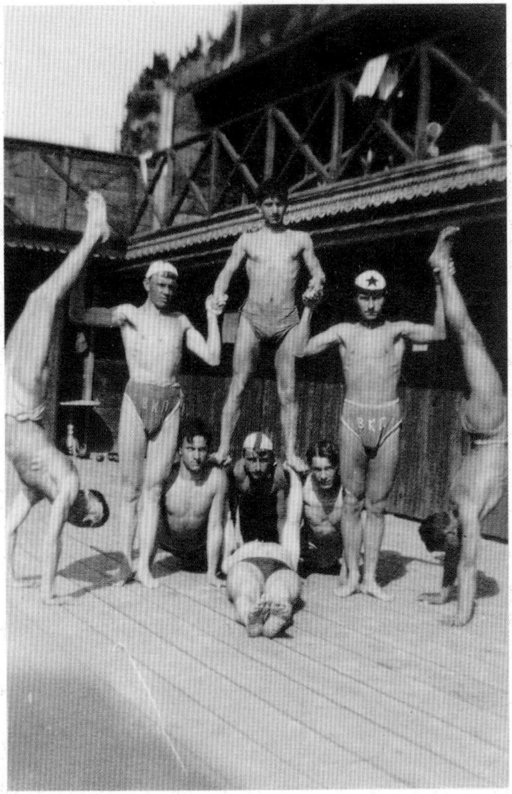

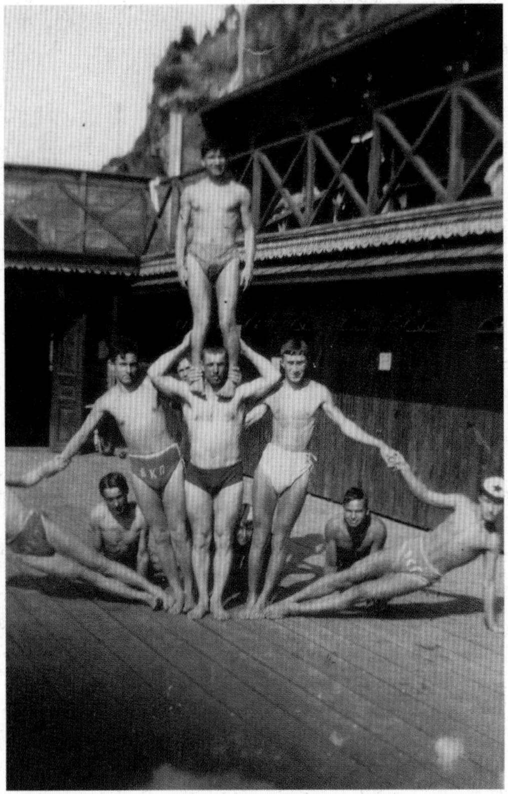

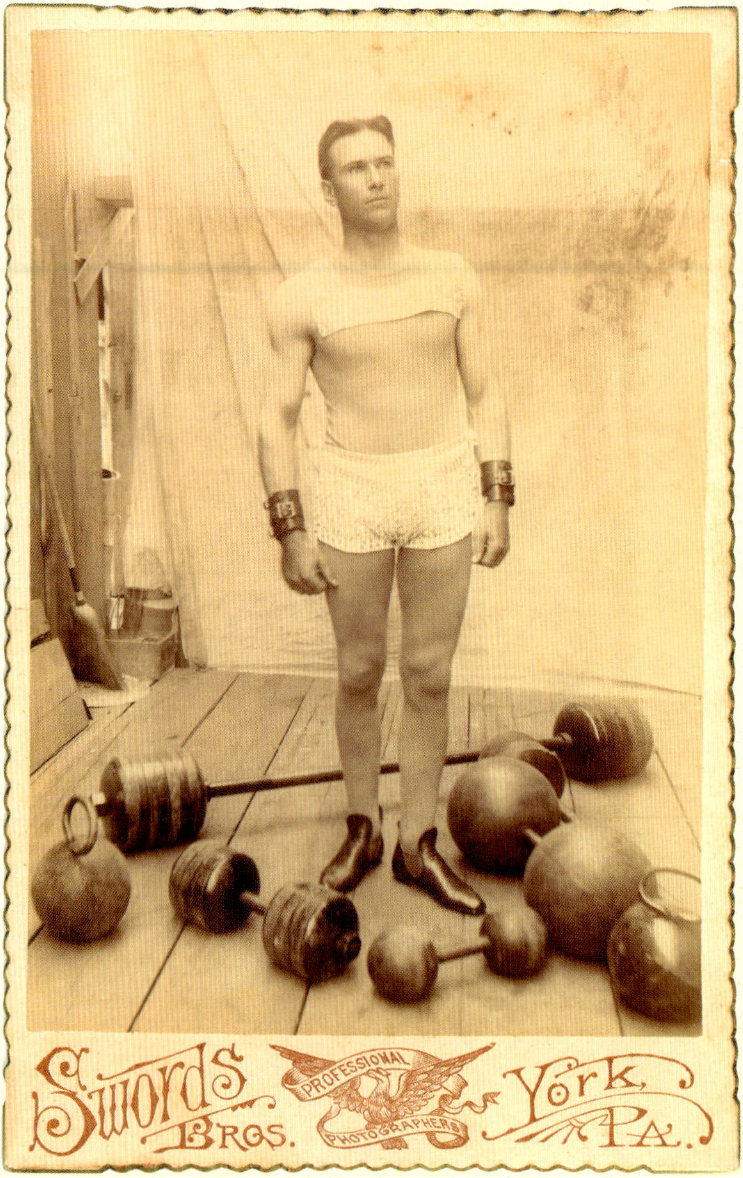

Harry H. Blowdell, Strongest American Living
by Sword Bros. York, Pa.
Cabinet card, c. 1890.

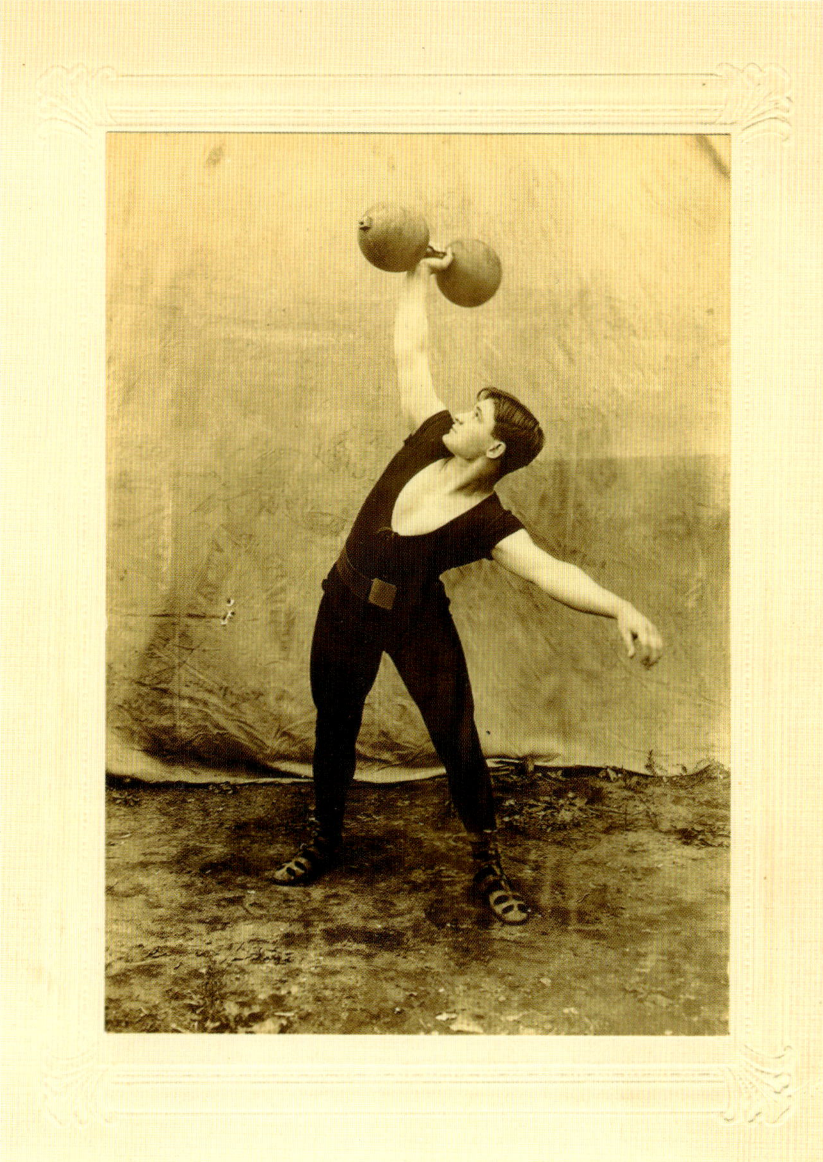

"My brother Joseph Tetreault, 17"
by John Warchol, Chicopee Falls, Mass.
Cabinet card, 1911.

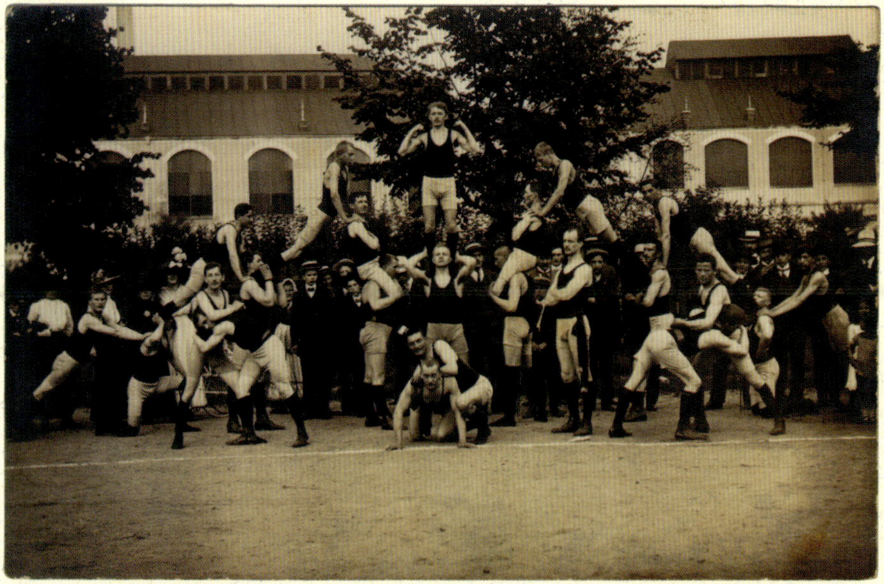

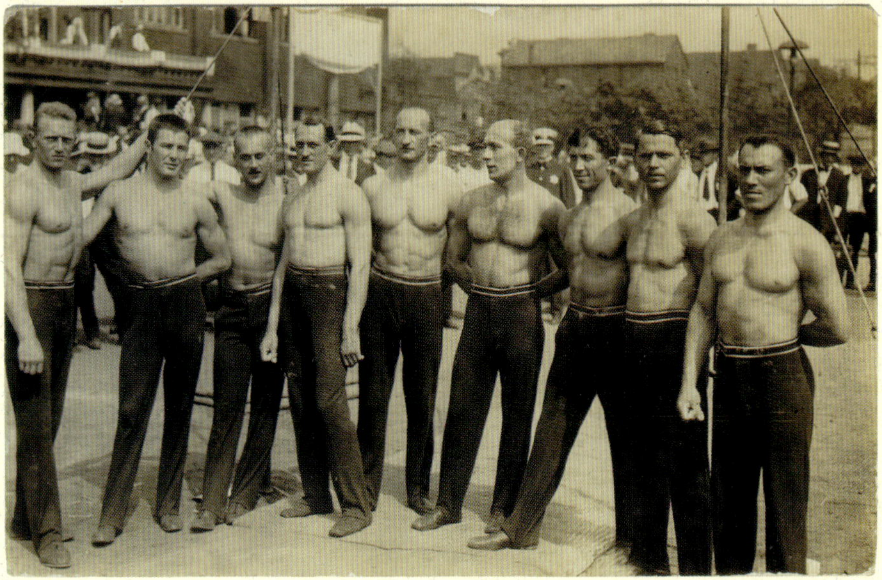

(Top) European athletic team. Postcard, c. 1920.
(Bottom) Anonymous Czech athletes.
American Postcard, 1921.

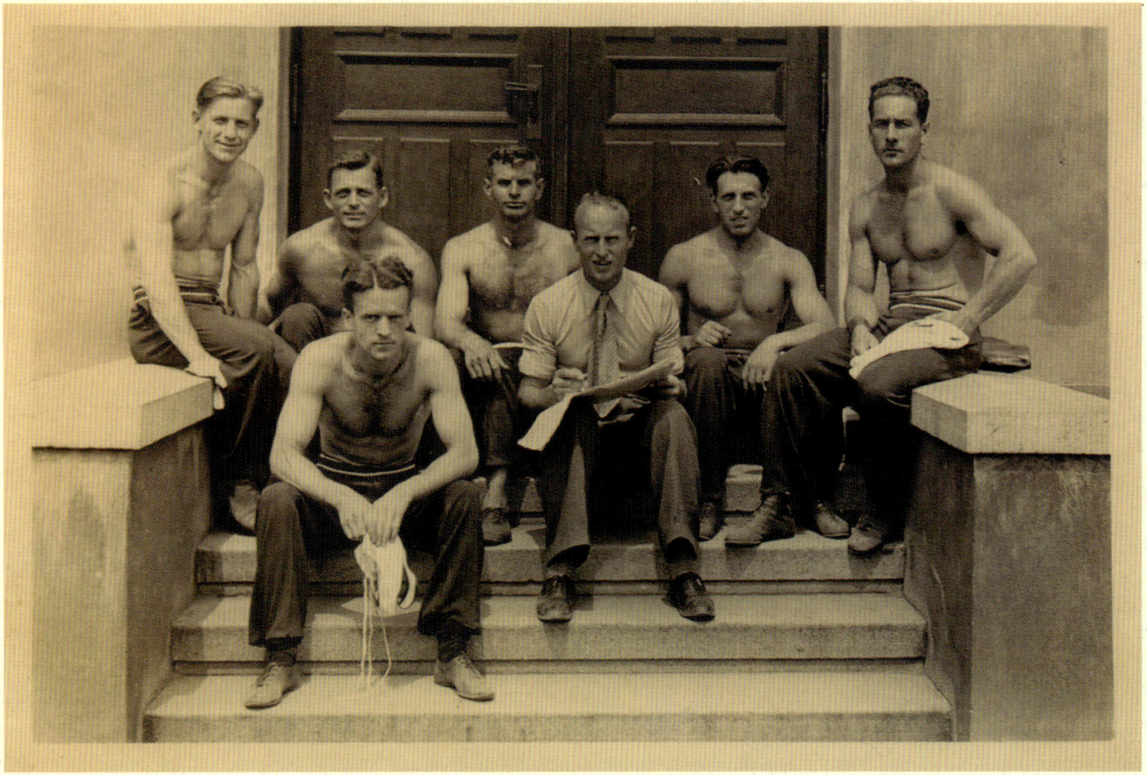

Anonymous Czech athletes.
Postcard, c. 1925.

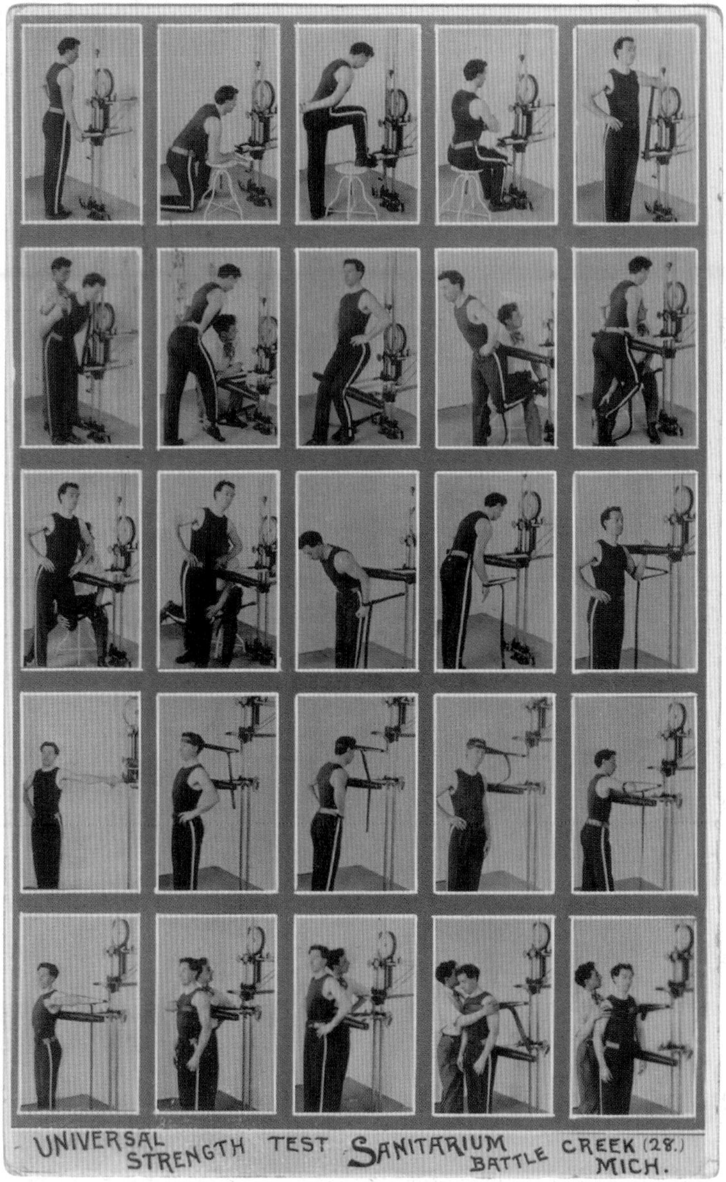

(Above) Sanitarium, Battle Creek, Mich. Postcard, 1911.
(Opposite) Emmett Faris, Cincinnati, Ohio.
Unattributed snapshot, 1937.

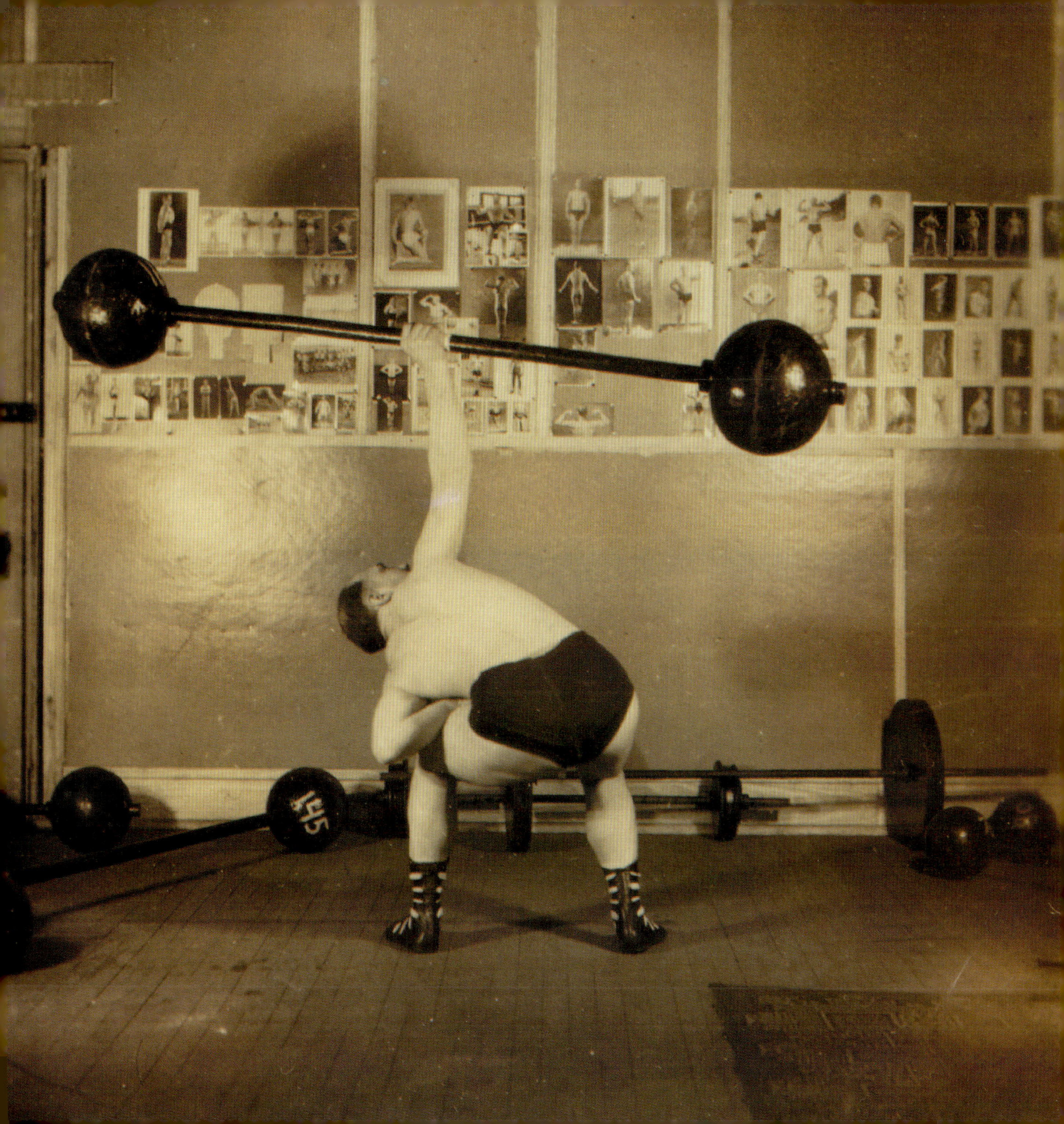
145

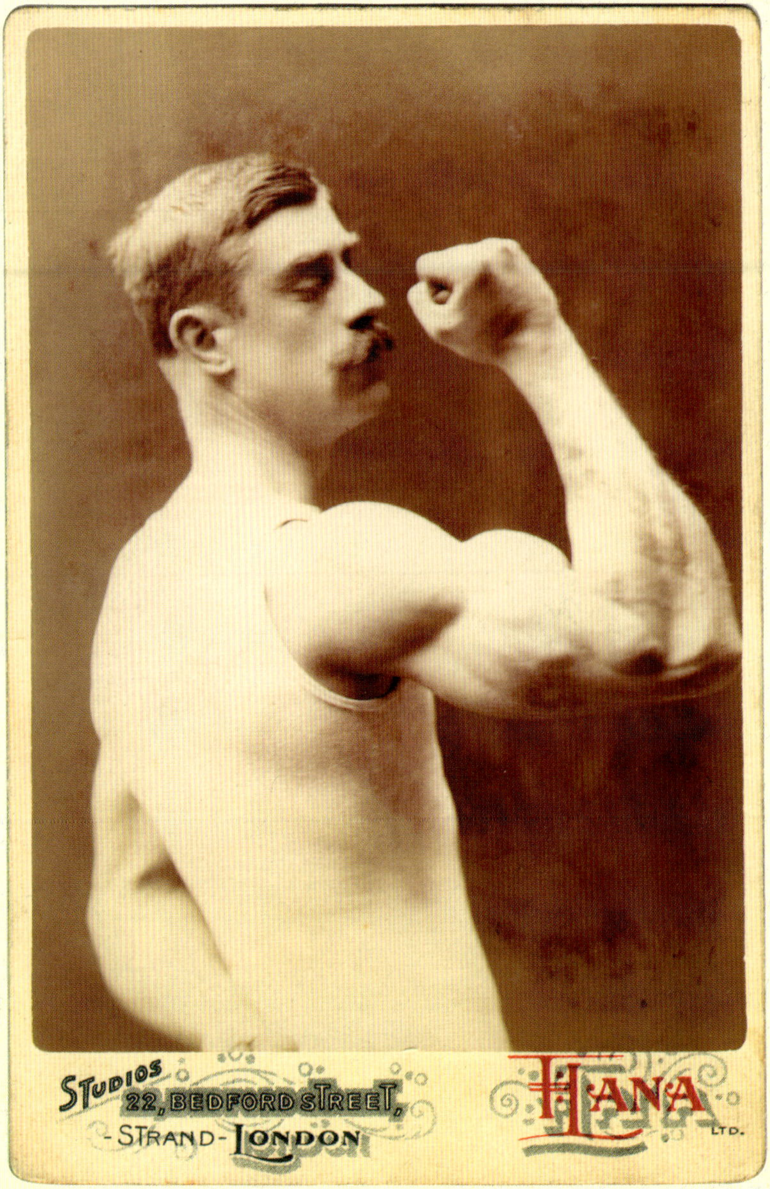

Charles Vansittart, The Man with the Iron Grip
by Hana, London. Cabinet card, c. 1900.

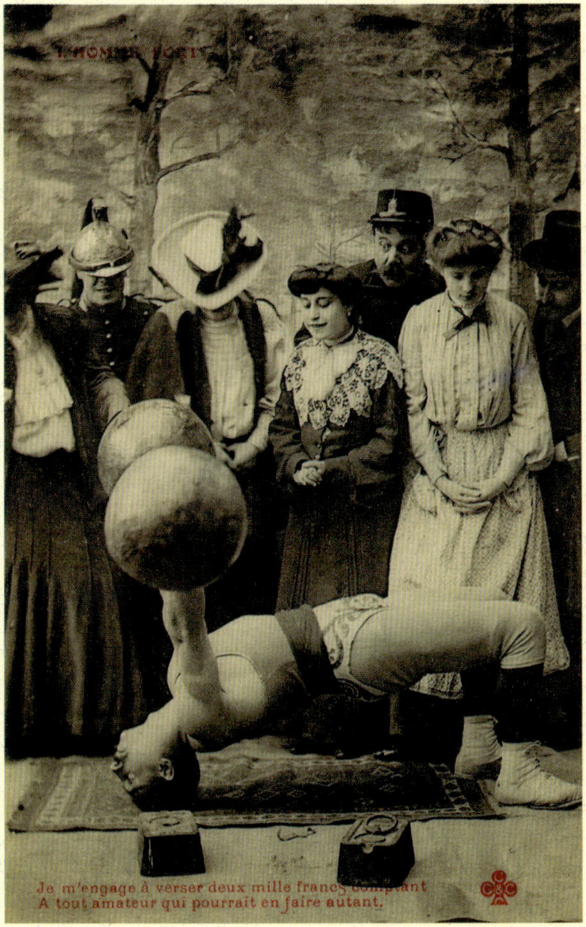

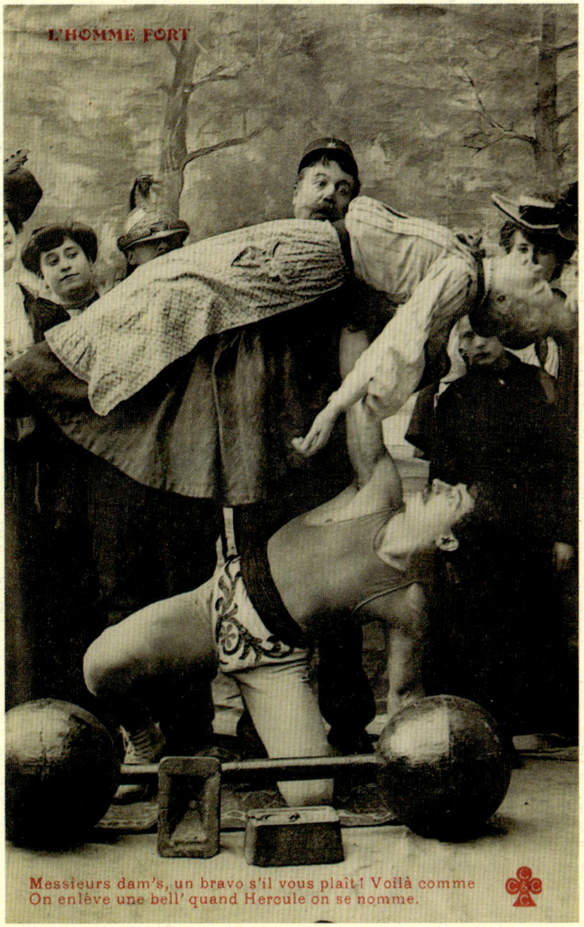

L'Homme Fort, from a series of six
French postcards, c. 1910.

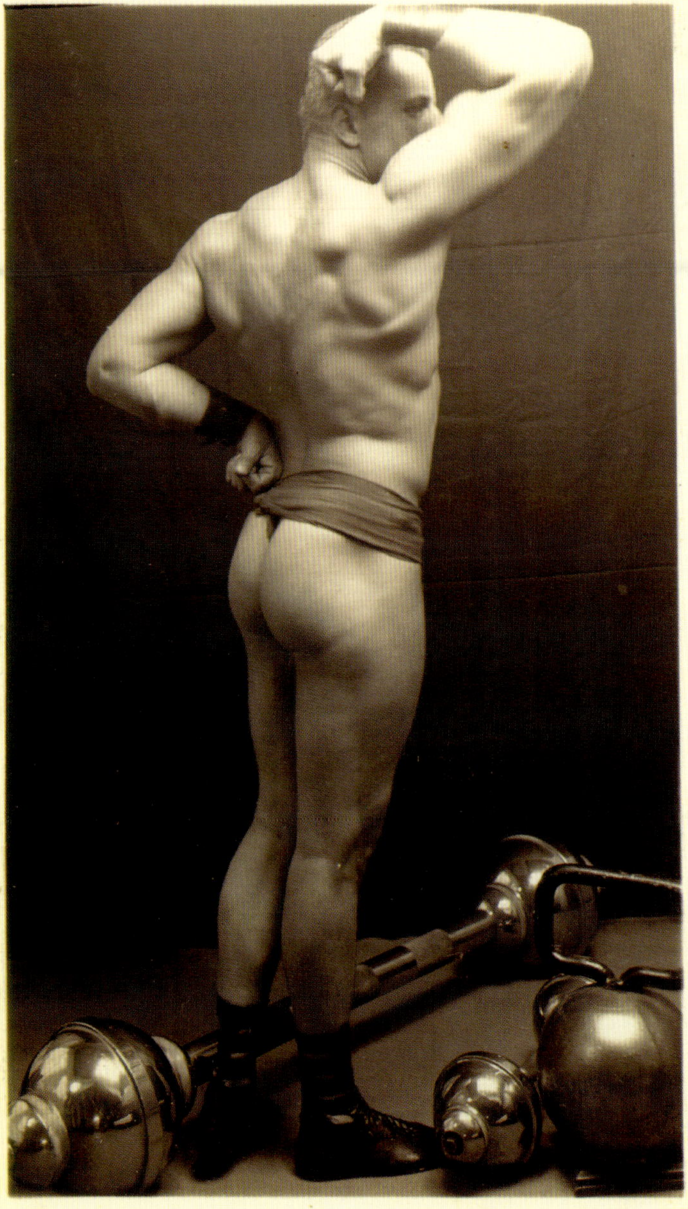

A. P. Hedlund, Minneapolis, Minn.
Unattributed snapshot, c. 1915.

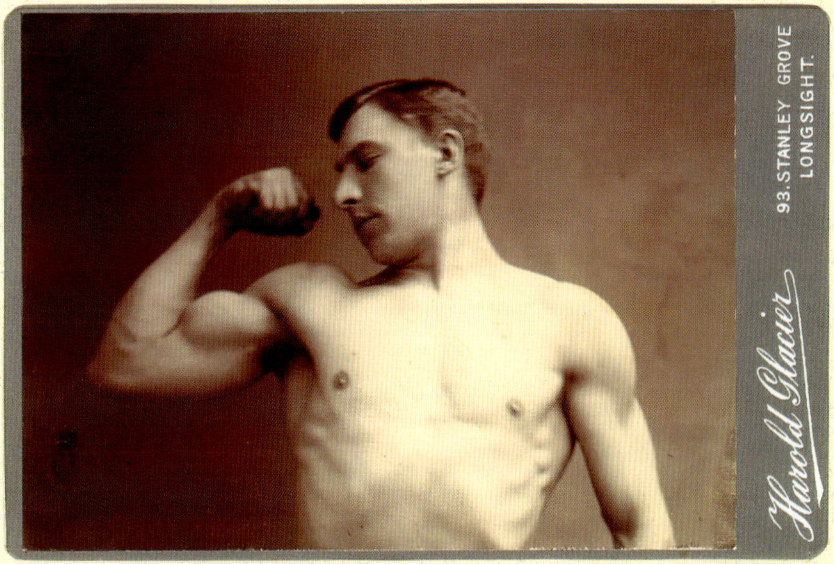

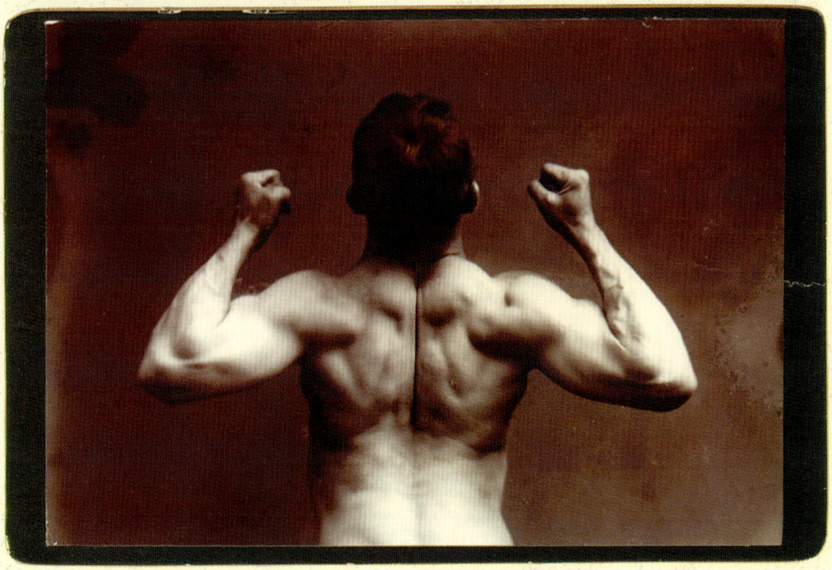

(Top) Unidentified strongman
by Glacier (British). Cabinet card, c. 1890.
(Bottom) Milo Brinn.
Unattributed cabinet card, c. 1895.

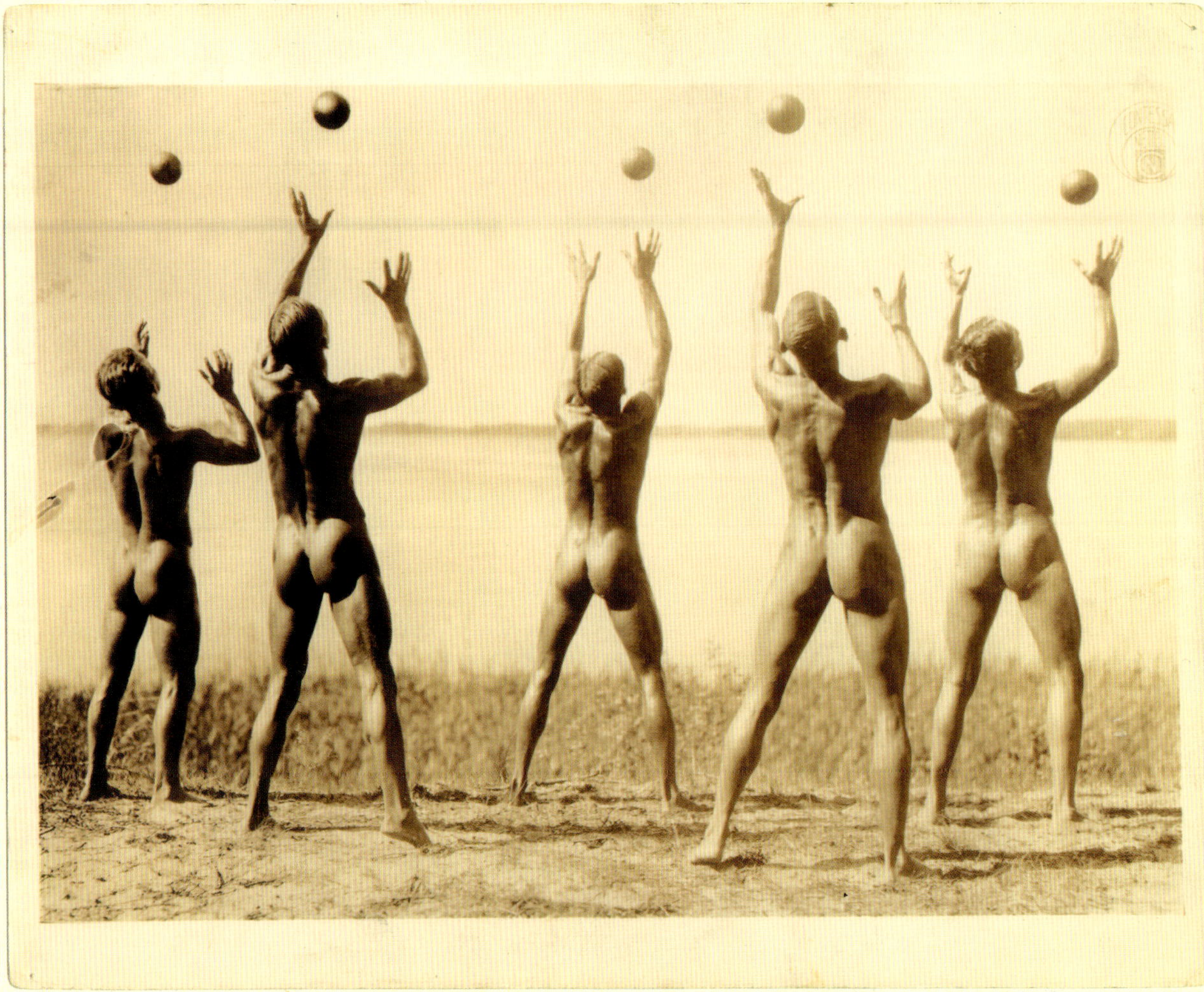

German Naturists (by Gerhard Riebicke?).
Silverprint, c. 1930.

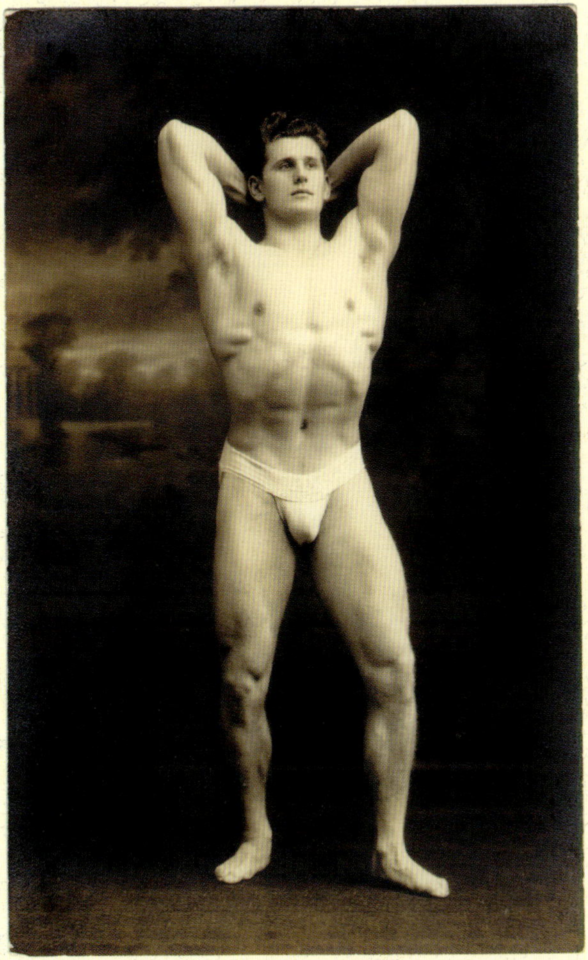

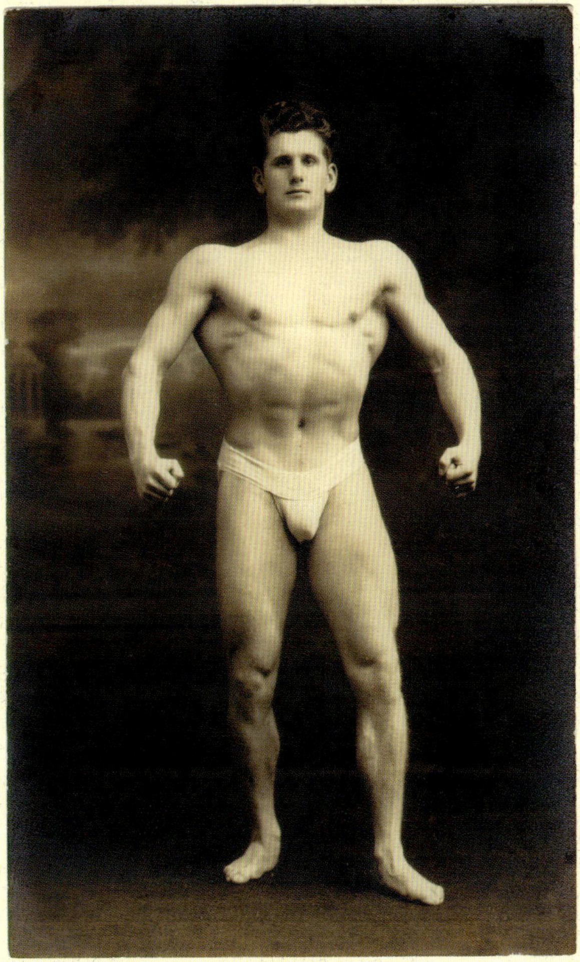

Sigmund Podolak.
Unattributed American postcards, 1935.

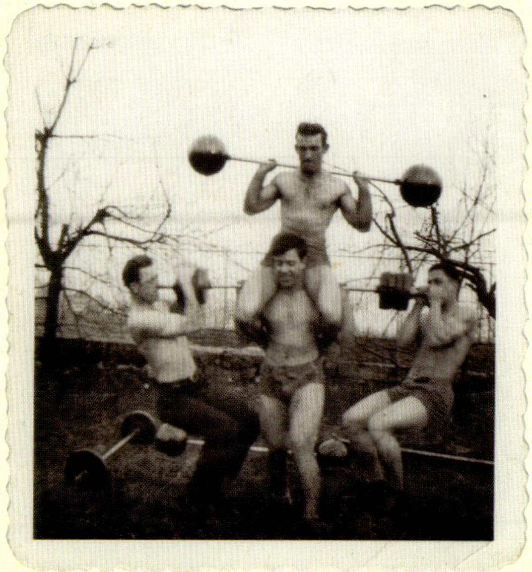

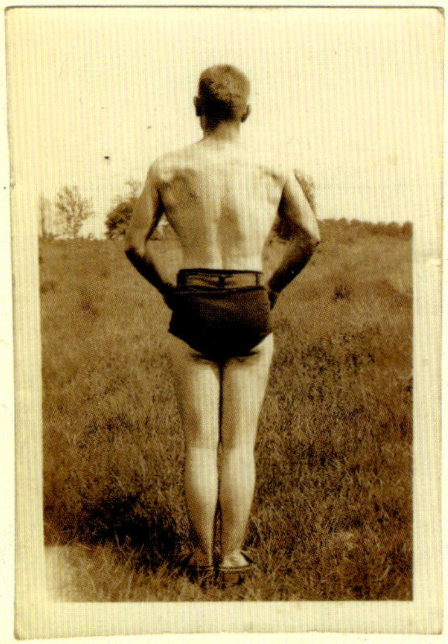

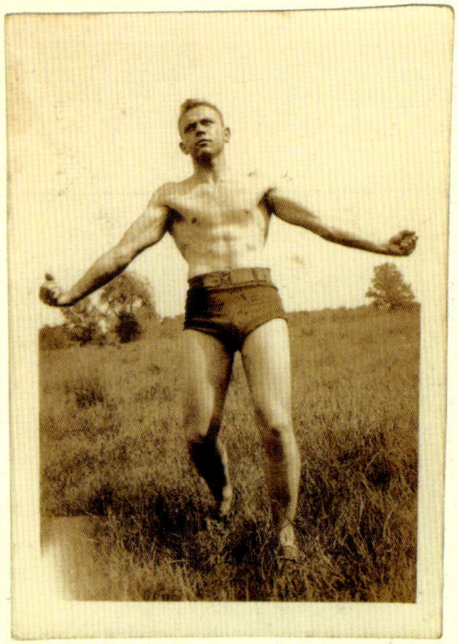

(*Top*) Anonymous snapshot, c. 1935.
(*Bottom*) Anonymous snapshots, 1935.

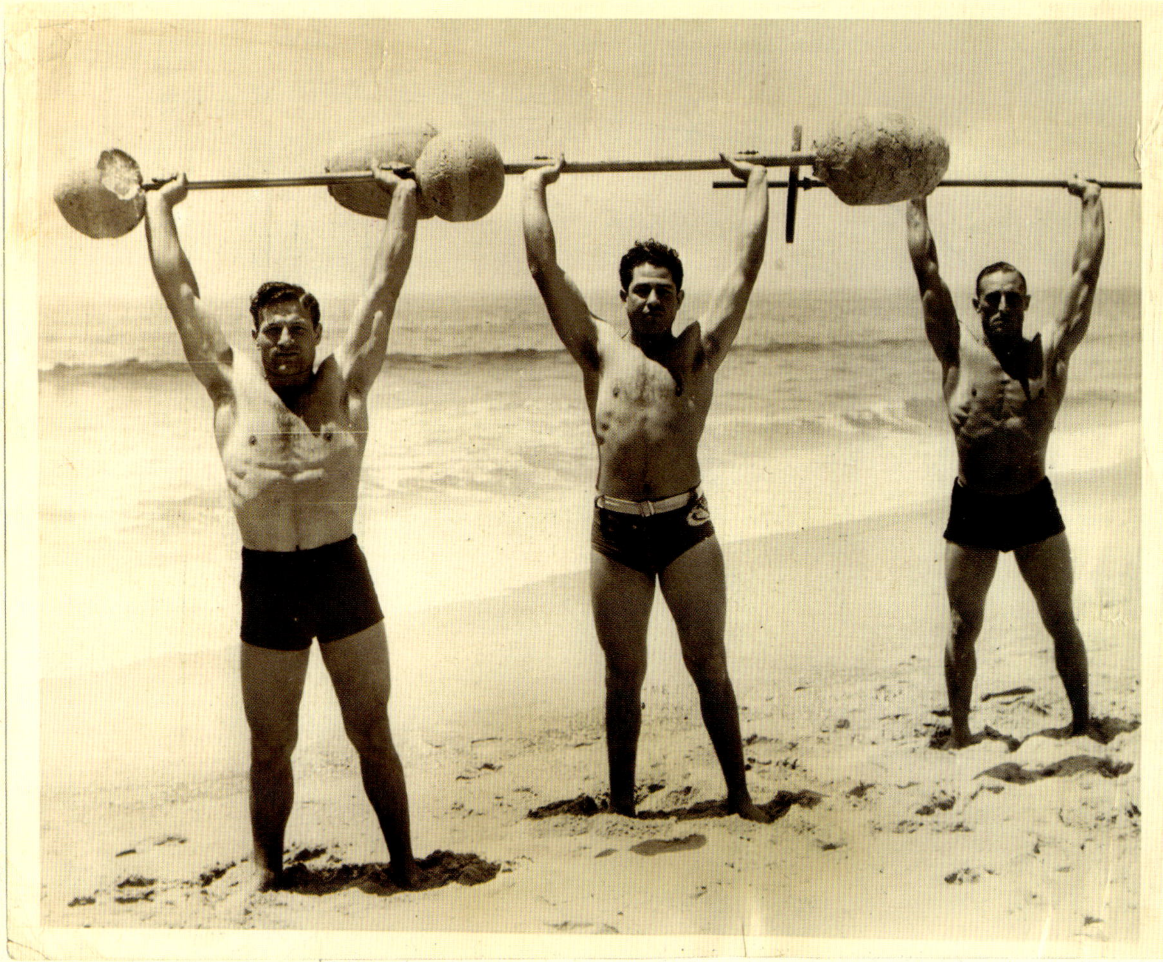

Sam Turmine, Maurice Aroff and Leonard Welte, Ocean Park, Calif.
Press photo by Acme/Trampus, 1932.

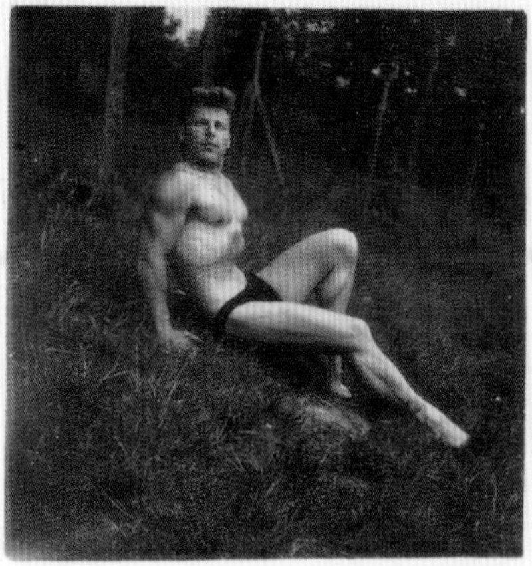

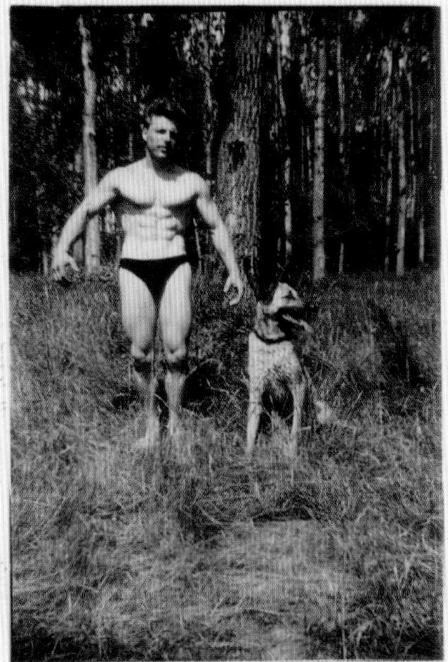

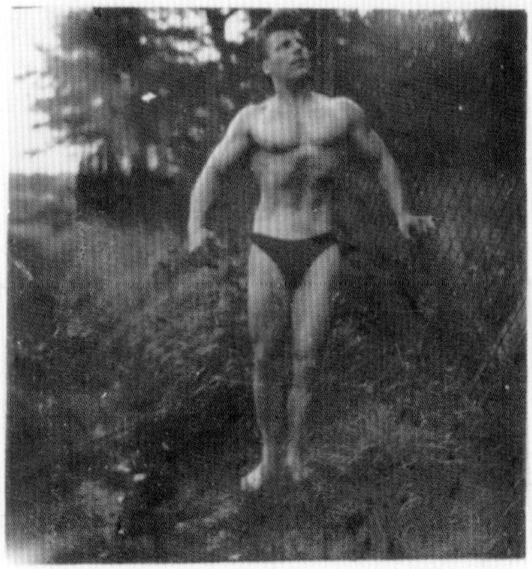

((Above) Norbert Wallet, Le Raincy, France.
Snapshots, 1953.
(Opposite) Desolation Valley.
American snapshot, c. 1935.

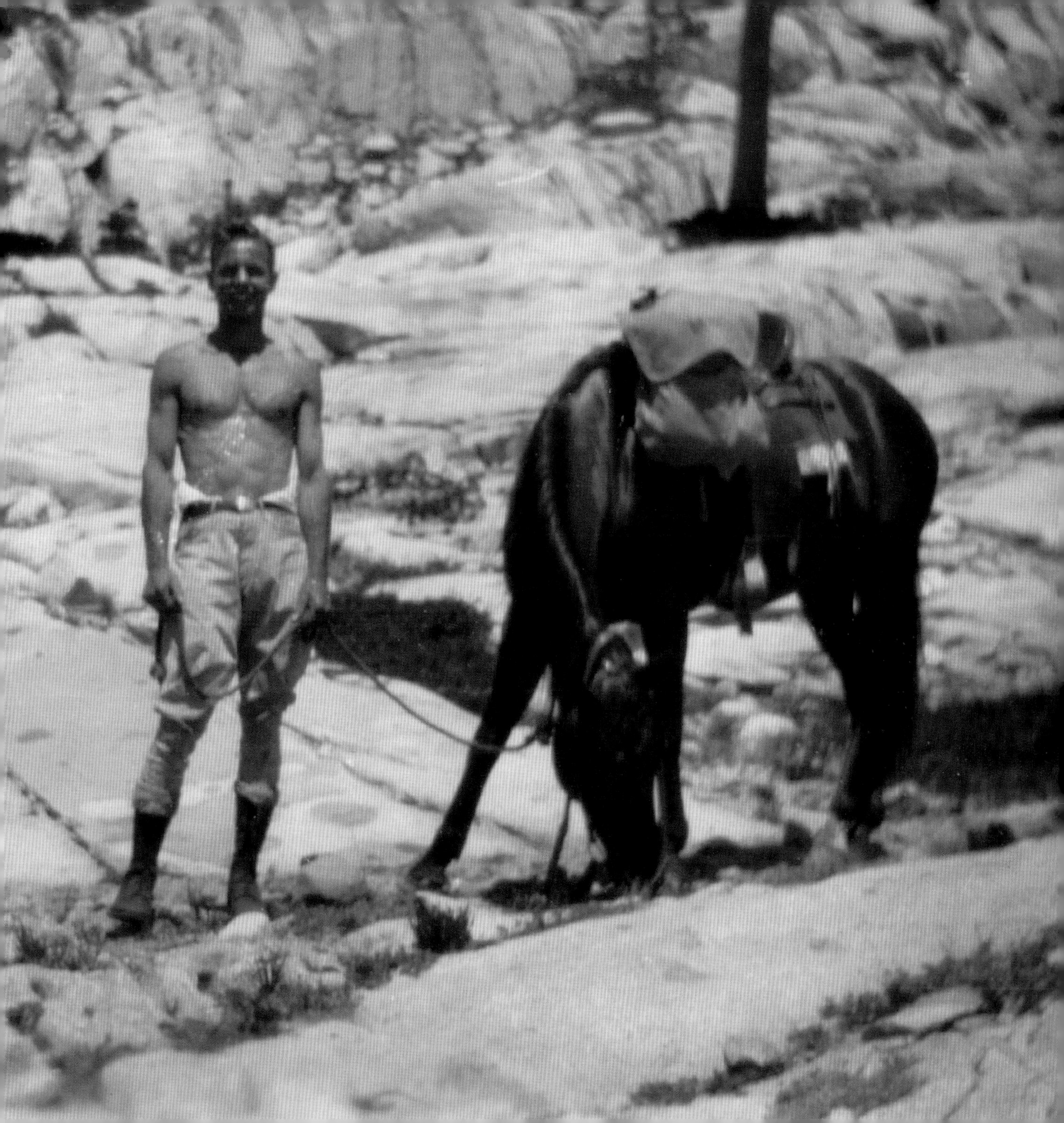

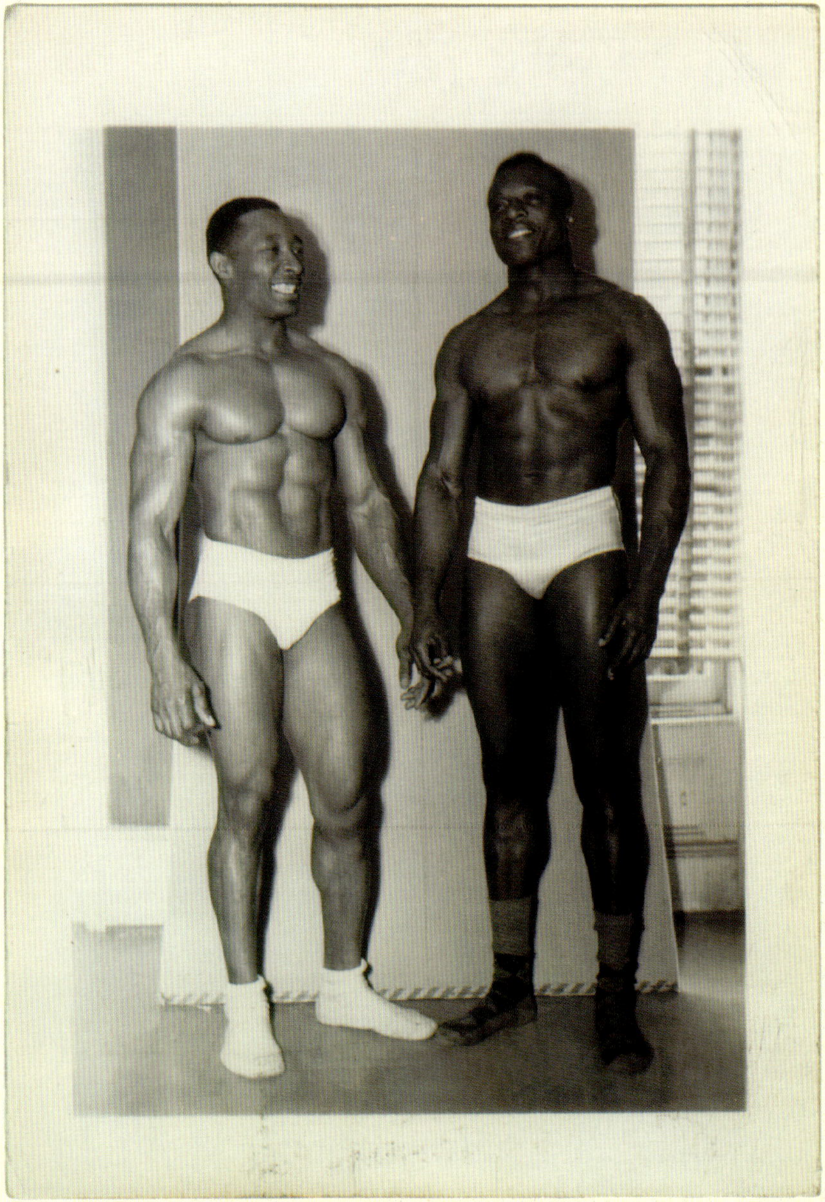

George Payne and unidentified model
by Lon Hanagan. Snapshot, c. 1950.

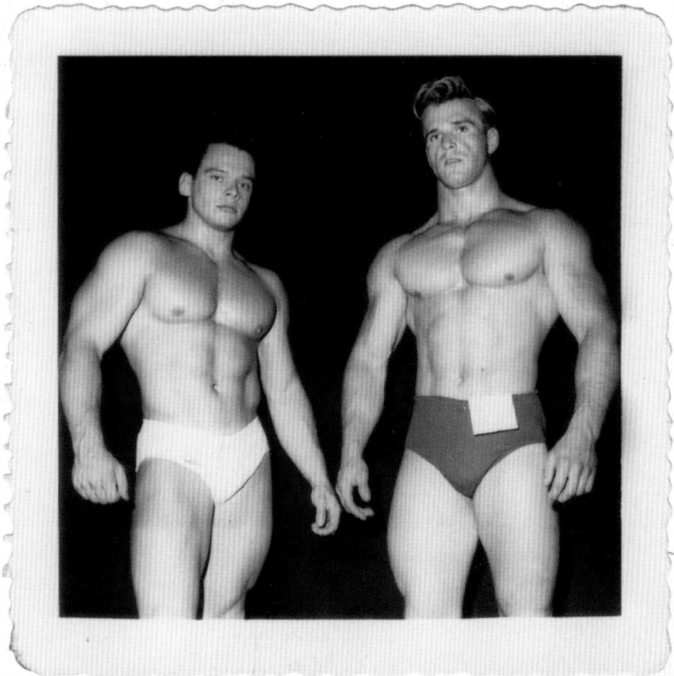

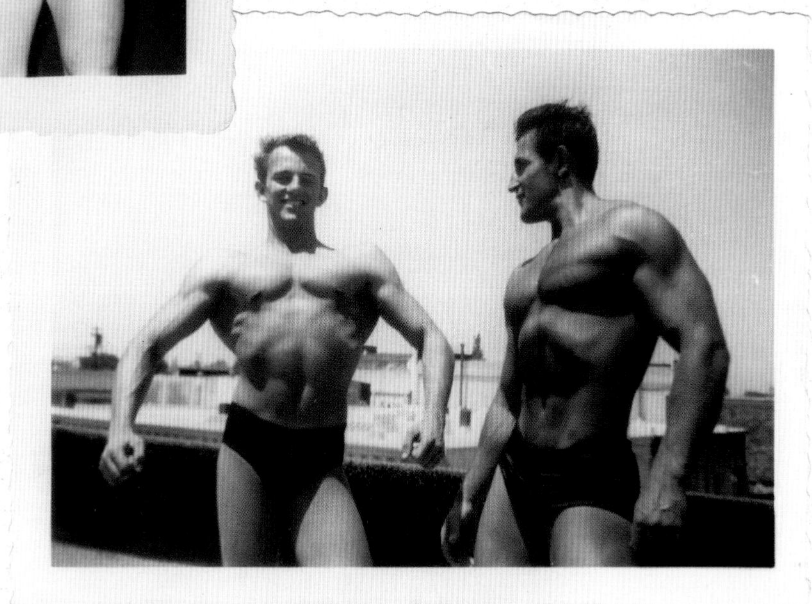

(Top) Dave Sheppard and Vic Seipke
by Douglas Juleff. Snapshot, c. 1948.
(Bottom) *Bob McCune* (right) *and unidentified model.*
Unattributed snapshot, c. 1948.

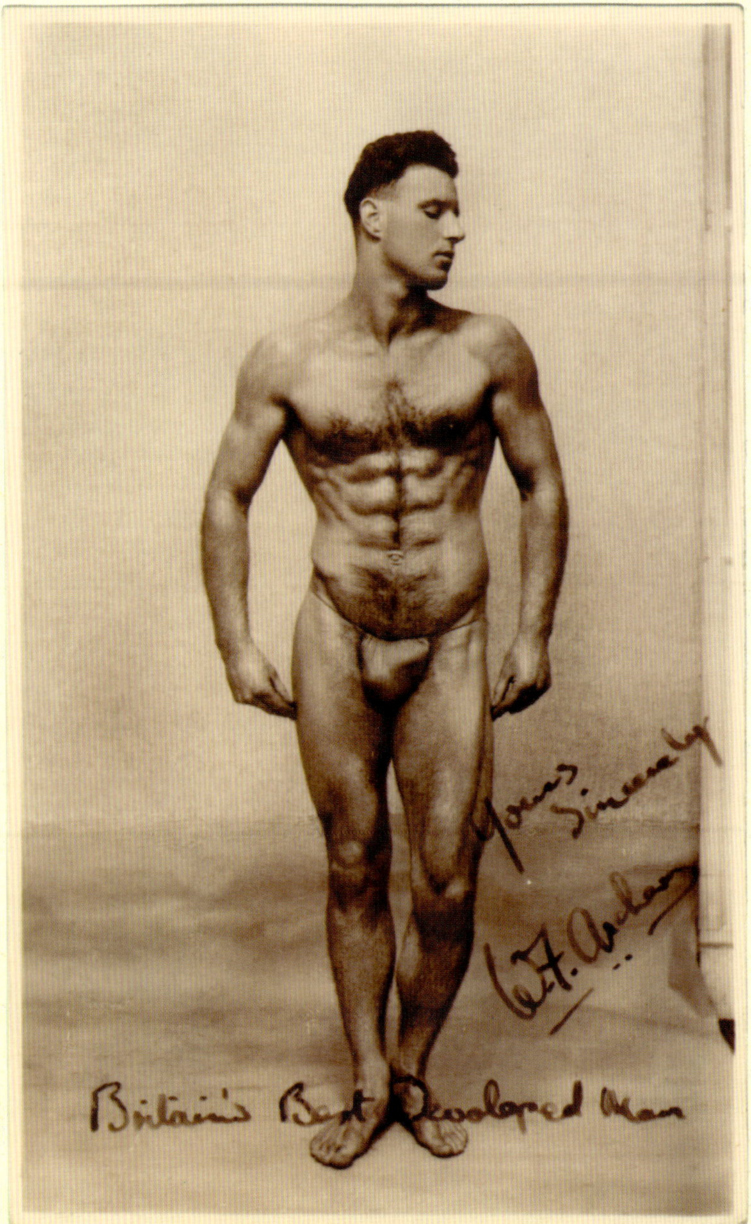

W. F. Archer, Britain's Best Developed Man.
Unattributed postcard, c. 1935.

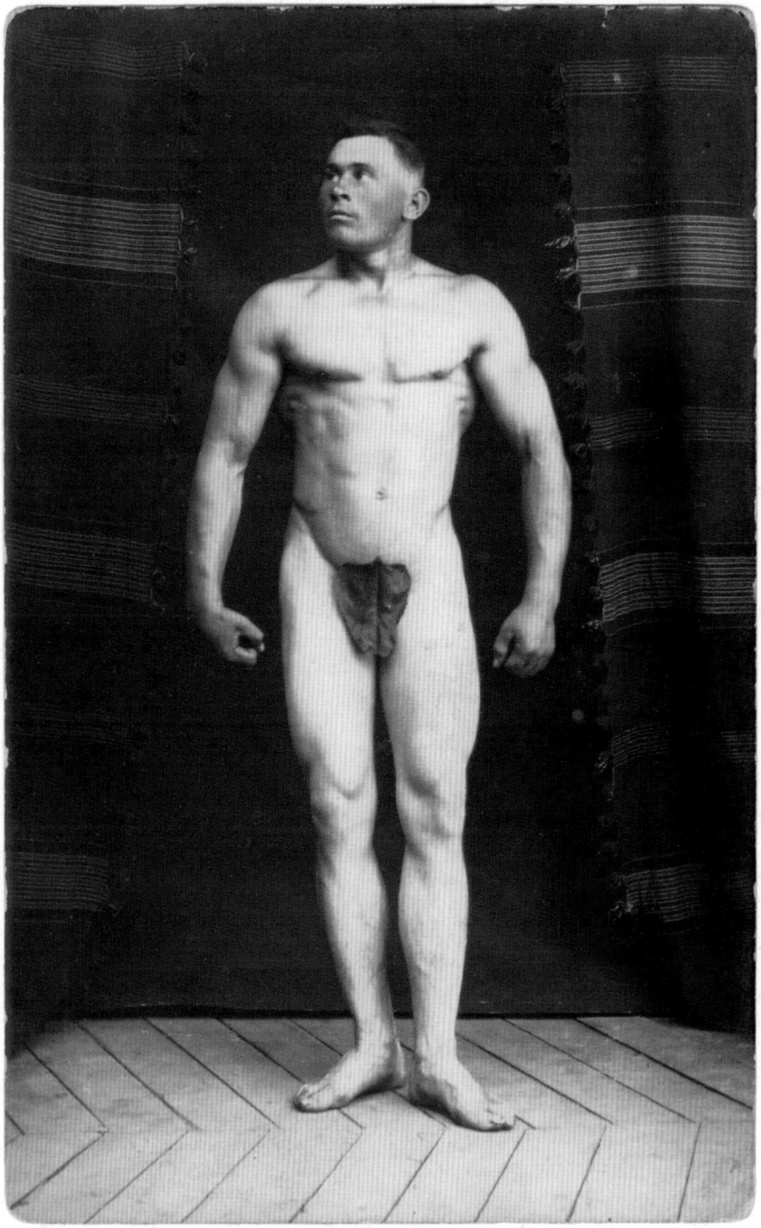

Anonymous Russian (?) postcard, c. 1925.

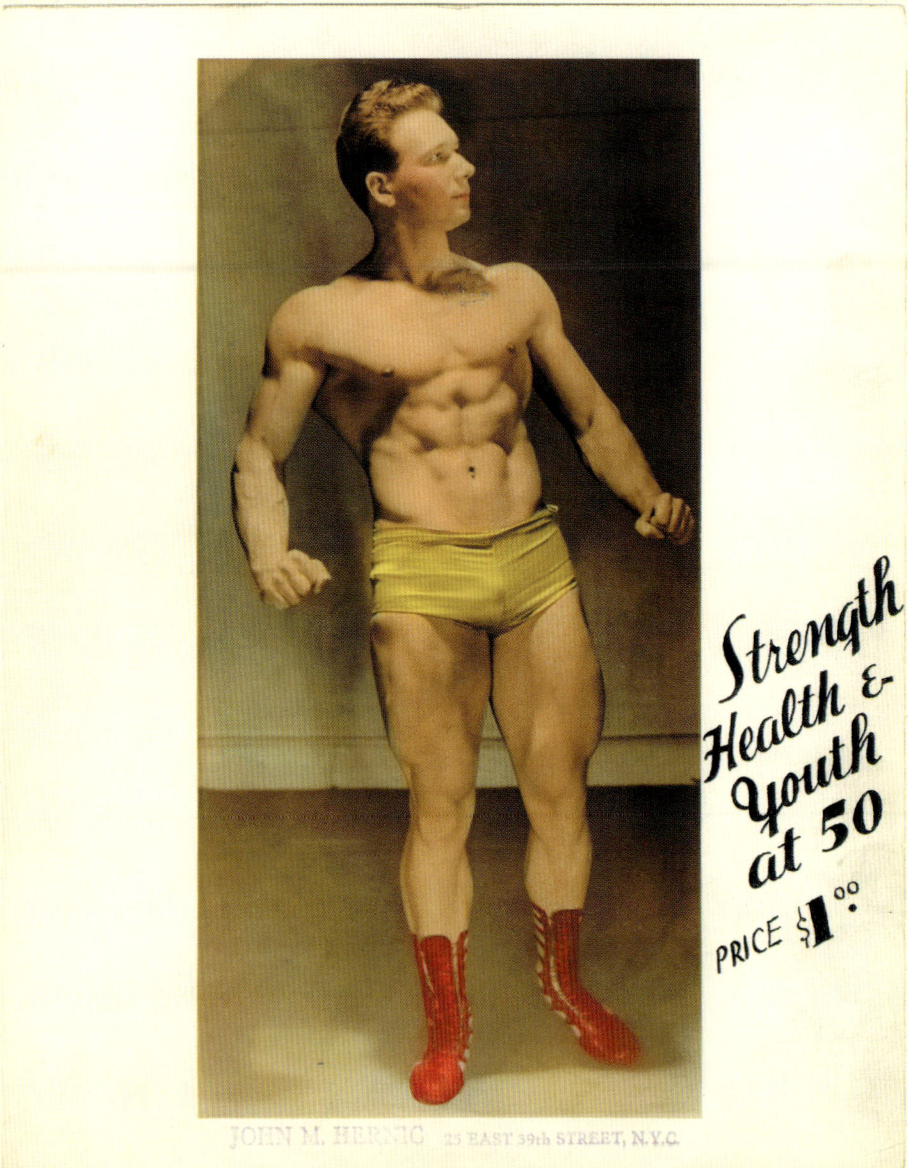

Barton Horvath by John M. Hernic.
Hand-colored advertising layout, c. 1936.

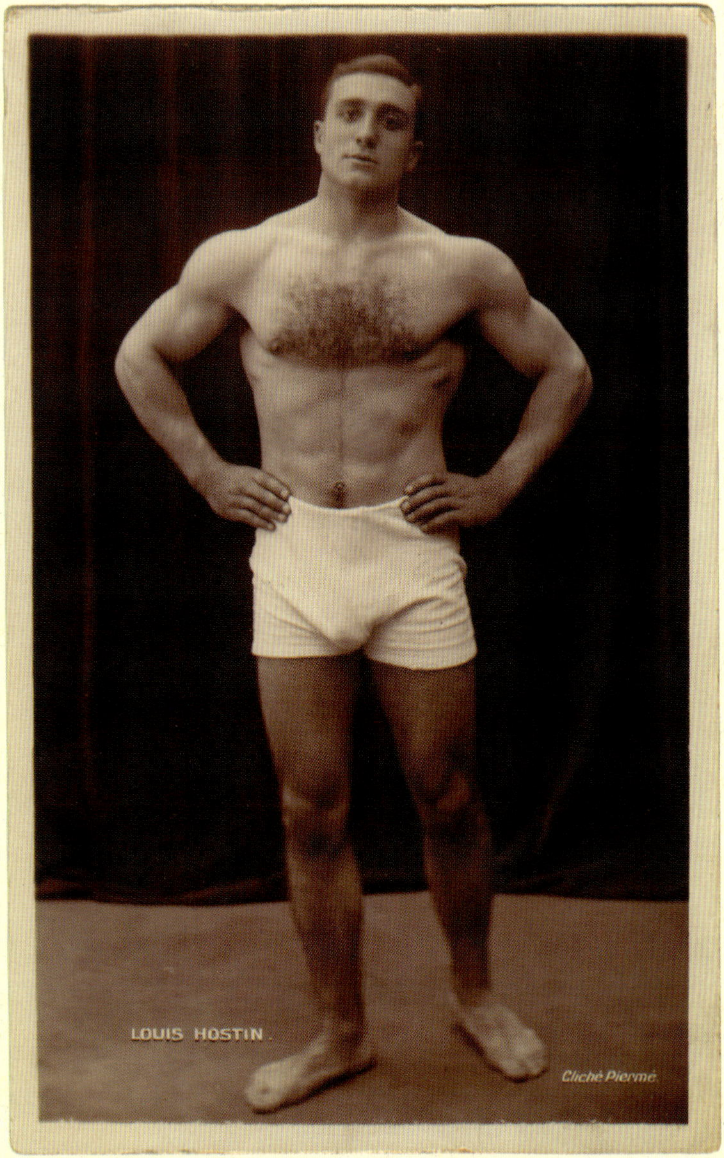

(Above) Louis Hostin. French postcard, c. 1930.
(Following pages) Military Gymnasium, Aldershot, England.
Underwood & Underwood stereoview, 1902.

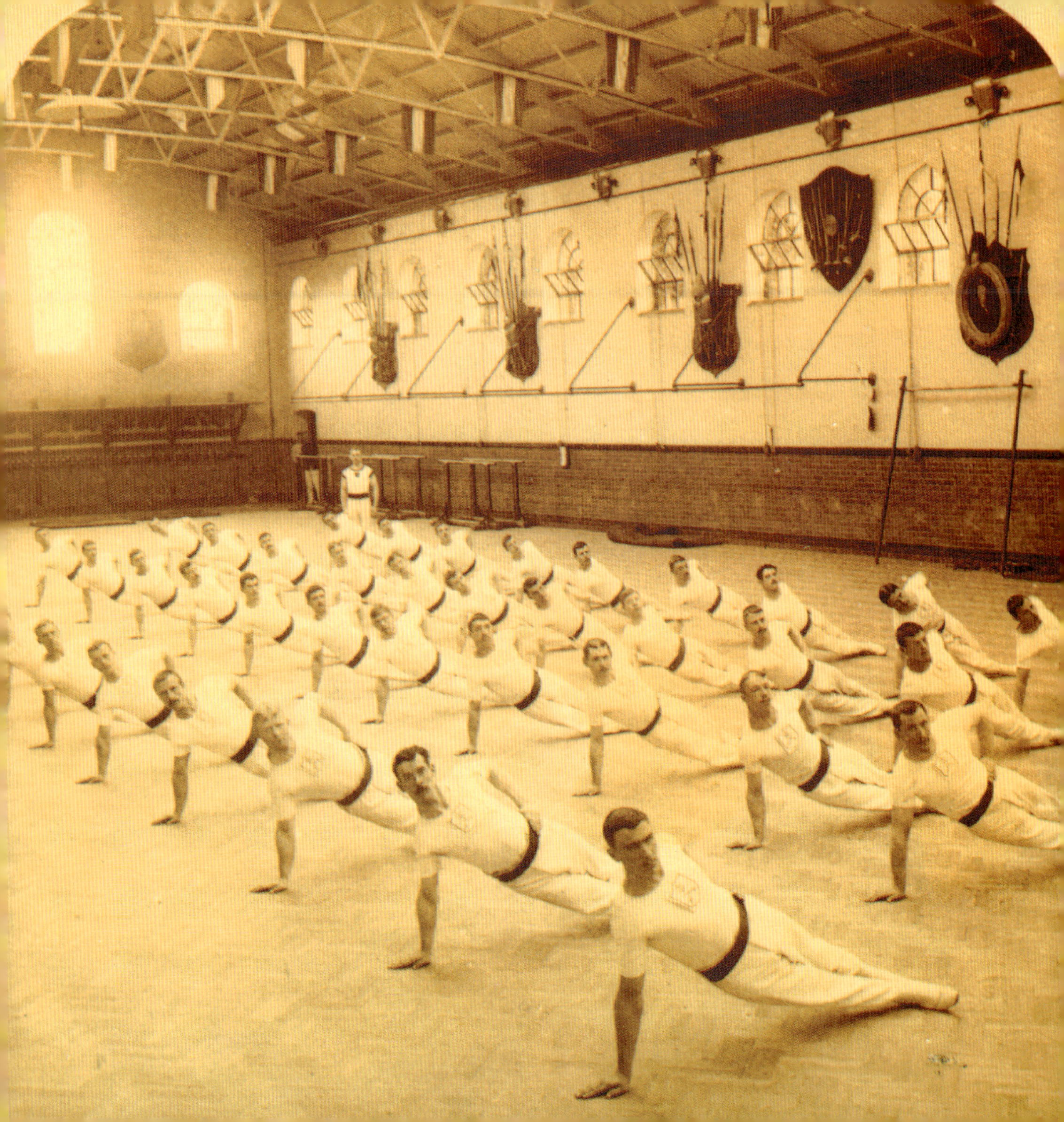

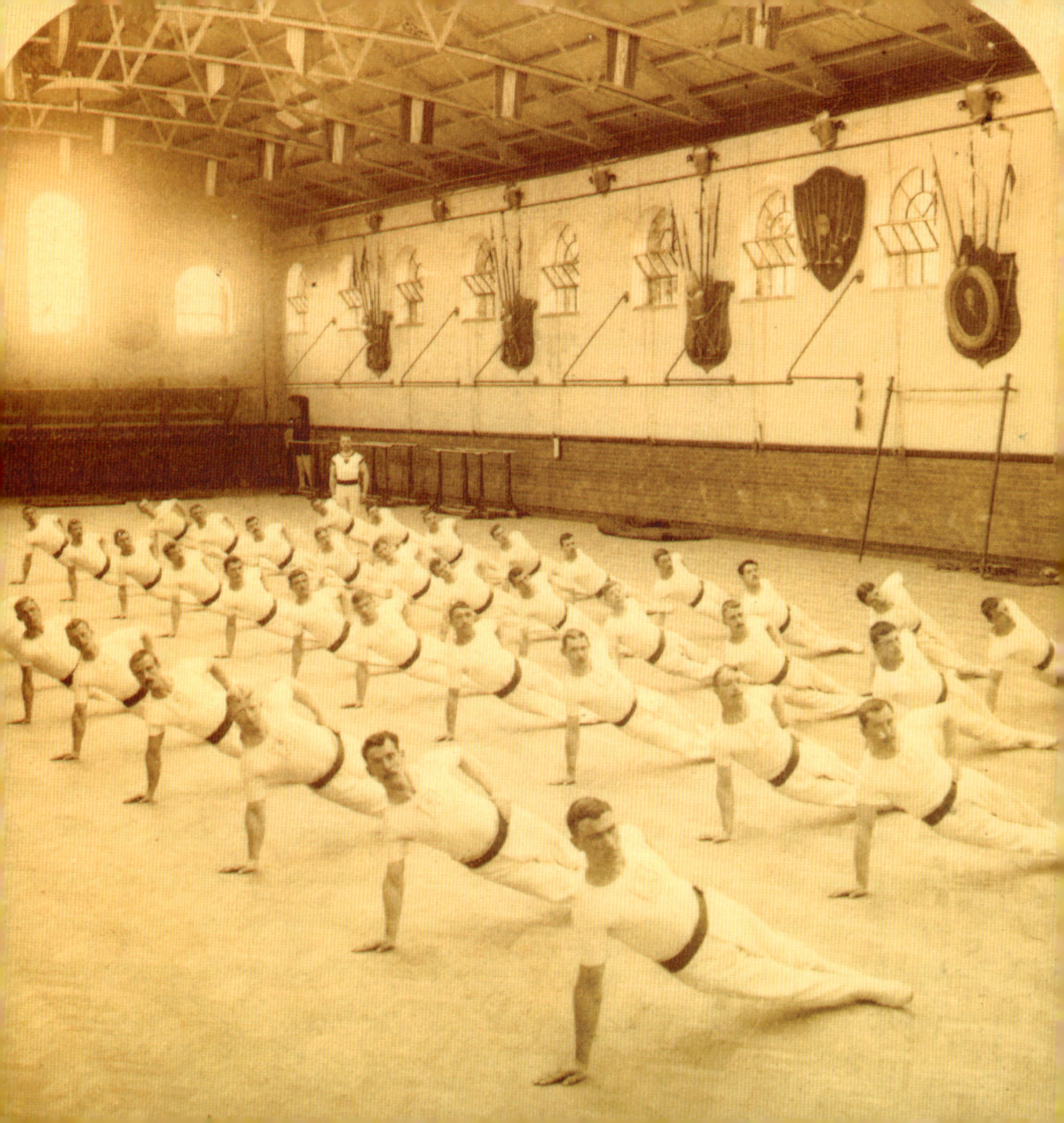

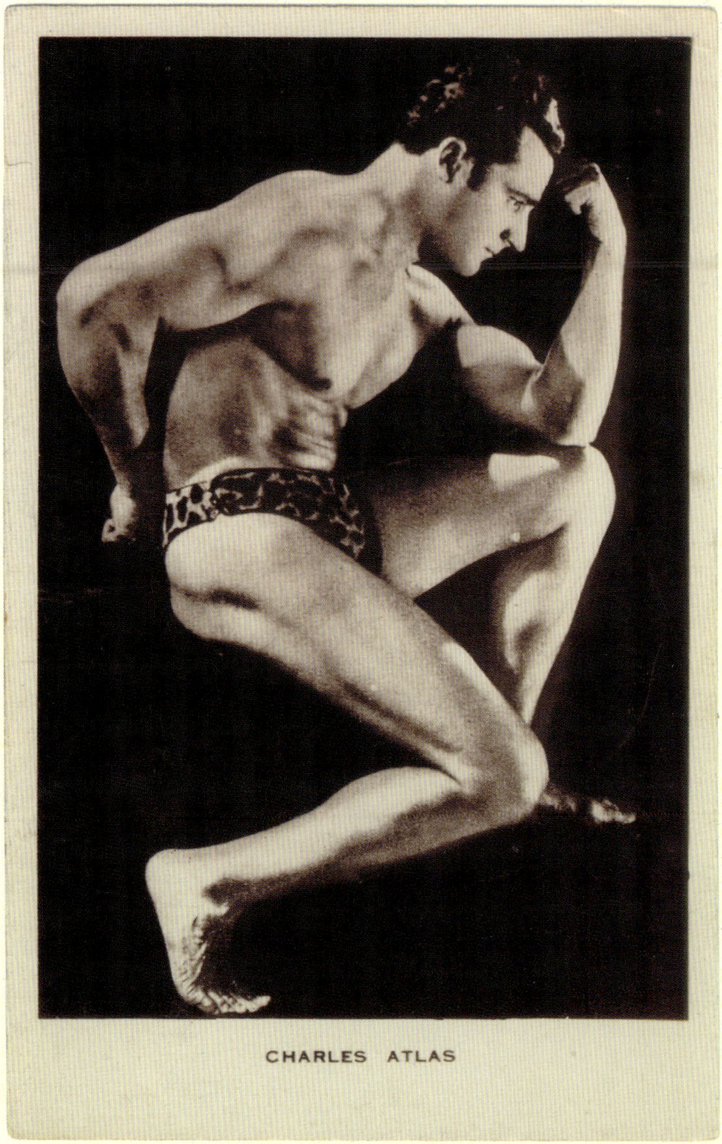

Charles Atlas (Angelo Siciliano), Italian immigrant, vaudeville strongman and mail-order entrepreneur
by Edwin Townsend (?).
French postcard, c. 1925.

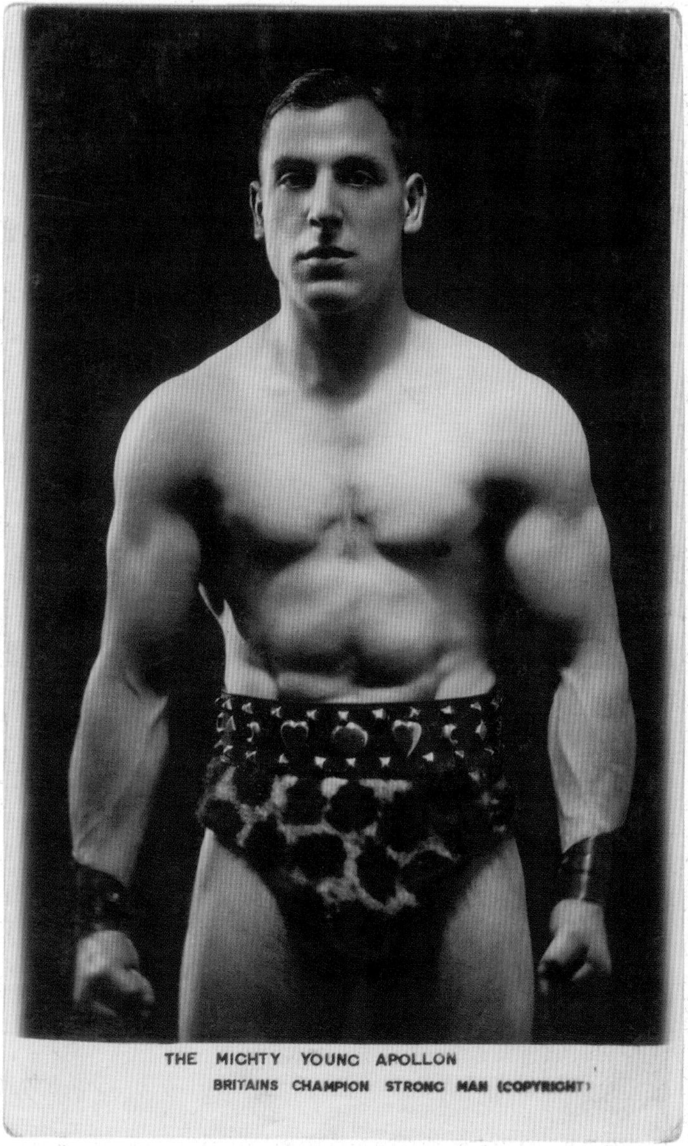

The Mighty Apollon, J. C. Tolson
by Borough Studio.
British postcard, c. 1925.

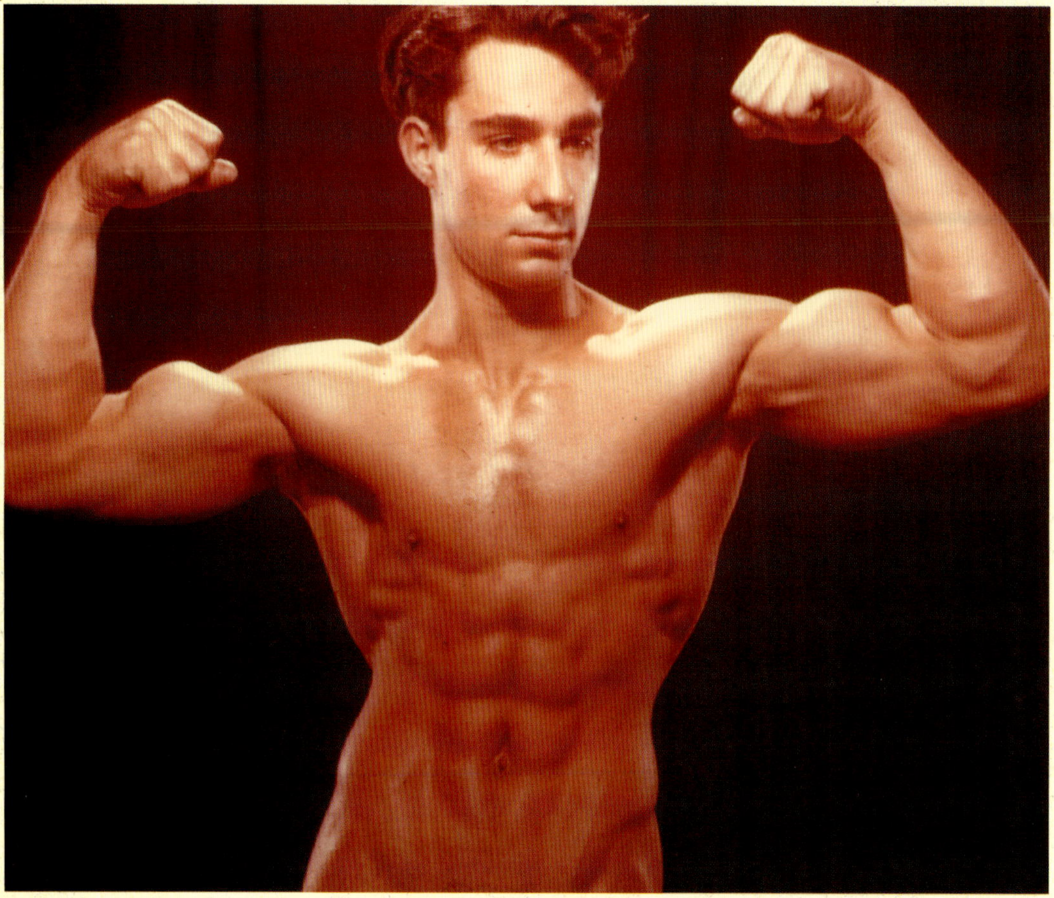

Frank Affrunti by Lon Hanagan.
Color photo, c. 1949.

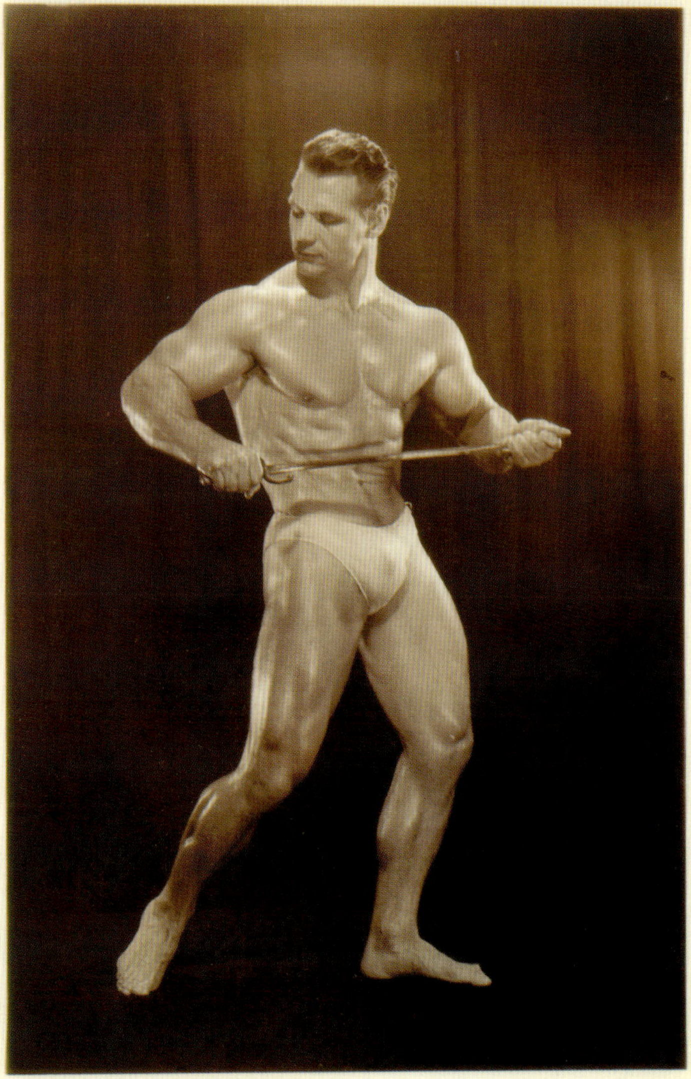

John Grimek, Mr. America 1940 and 1941,
Mr. Universe 1948, Olympic weightlifter
by Lon Hanagan. Silverprint, c. 1941.

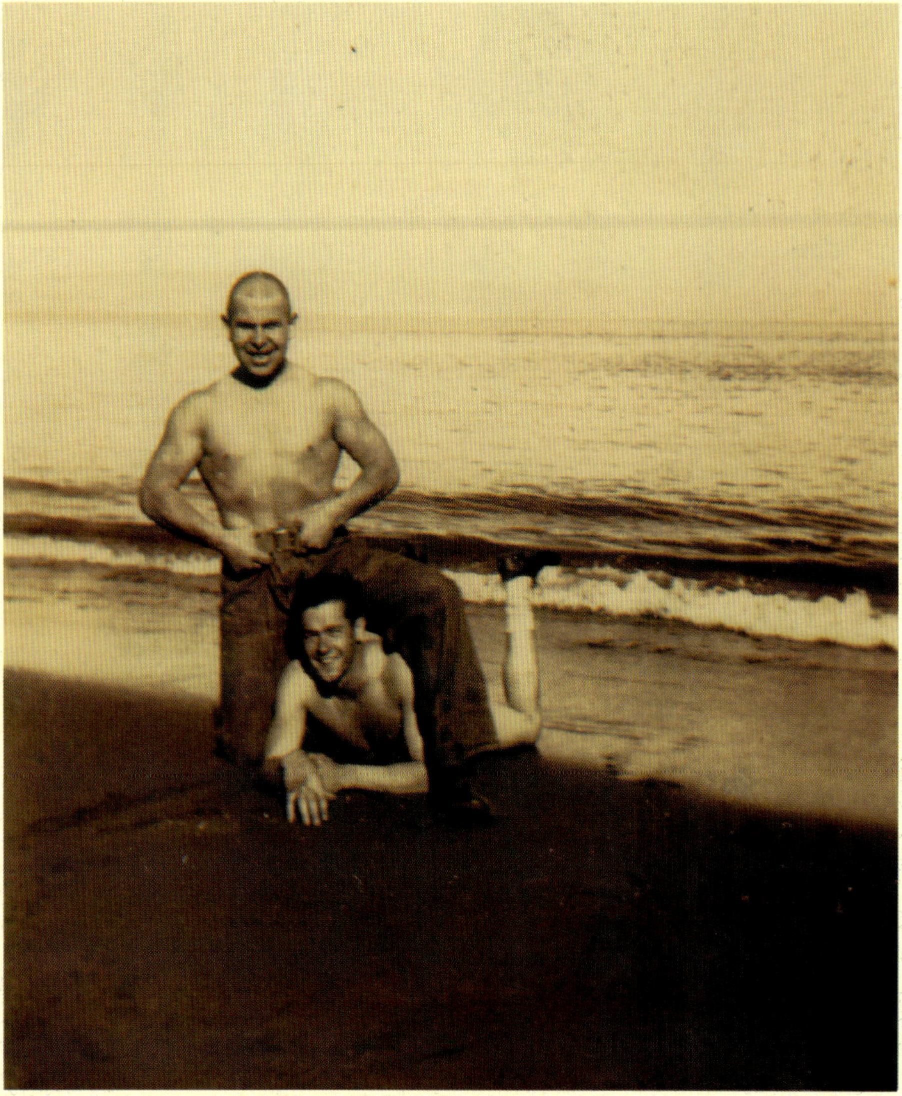

"Chessie, Frisco, My first Army haircut."
Snapshot, c. 1940.

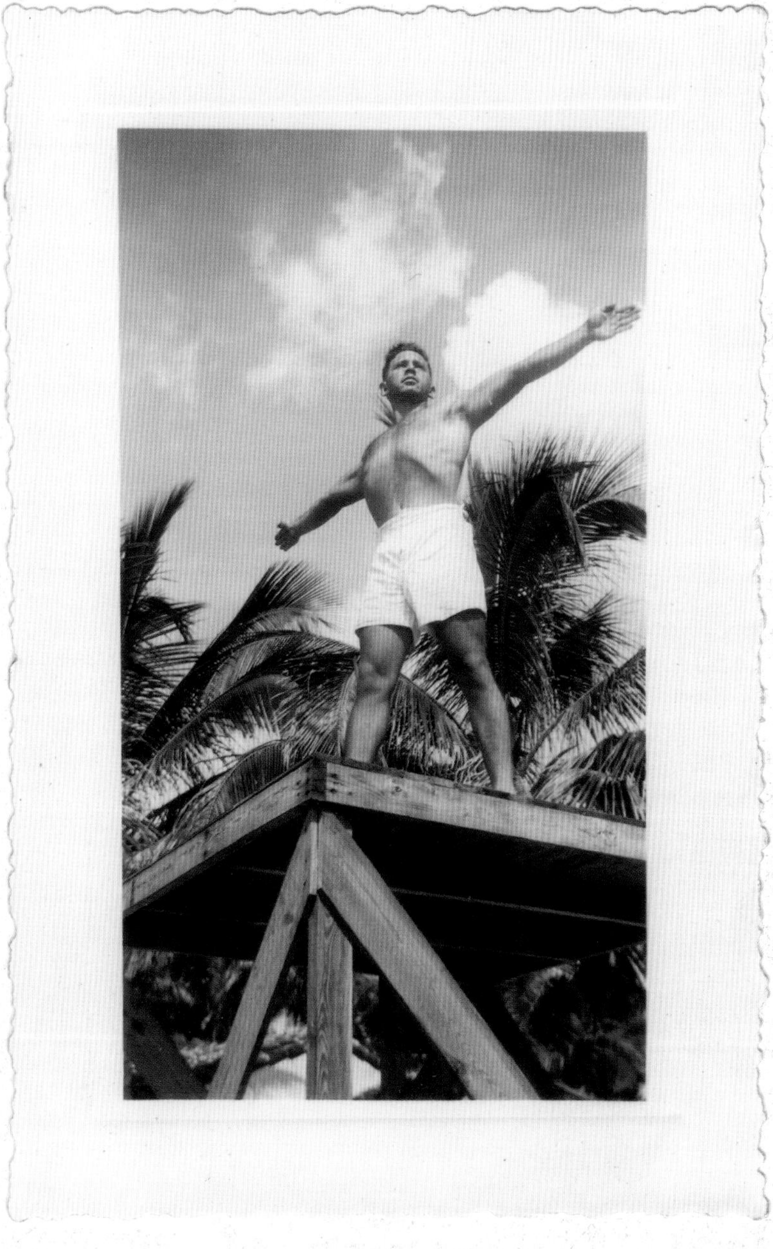

Anonymous snapshot, c. 1945.

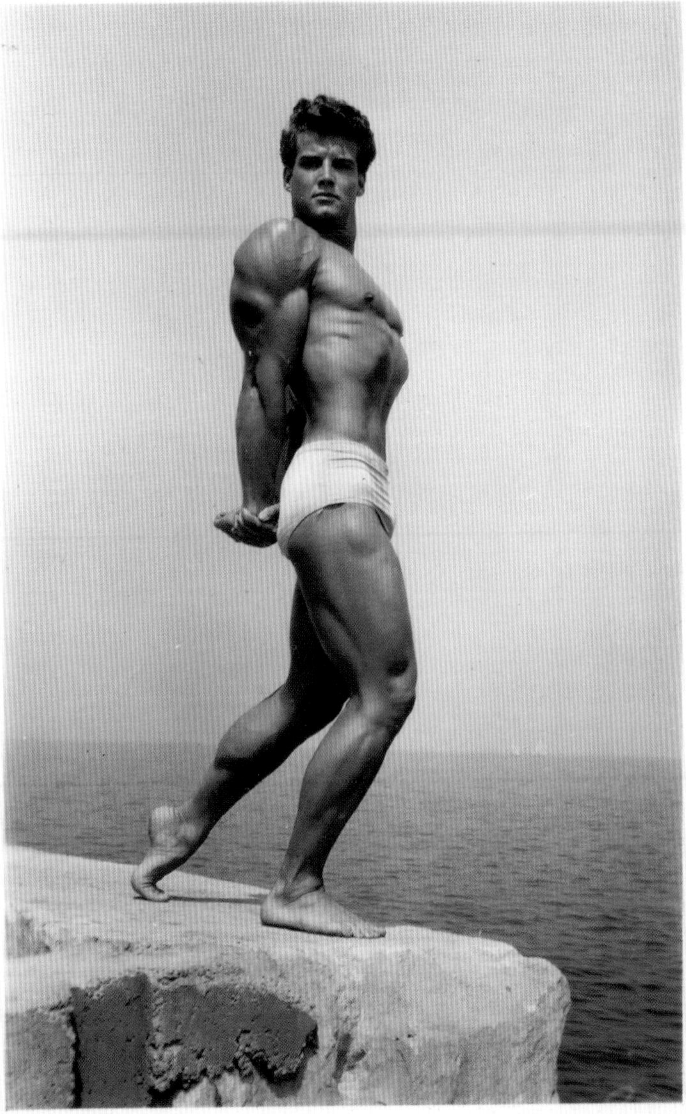

Steve Reeves, Mr. America 1947,
Mr. Universe 1948 and 1950, cinema Hercules
by Tony Lanza. Silverprint, 1947.

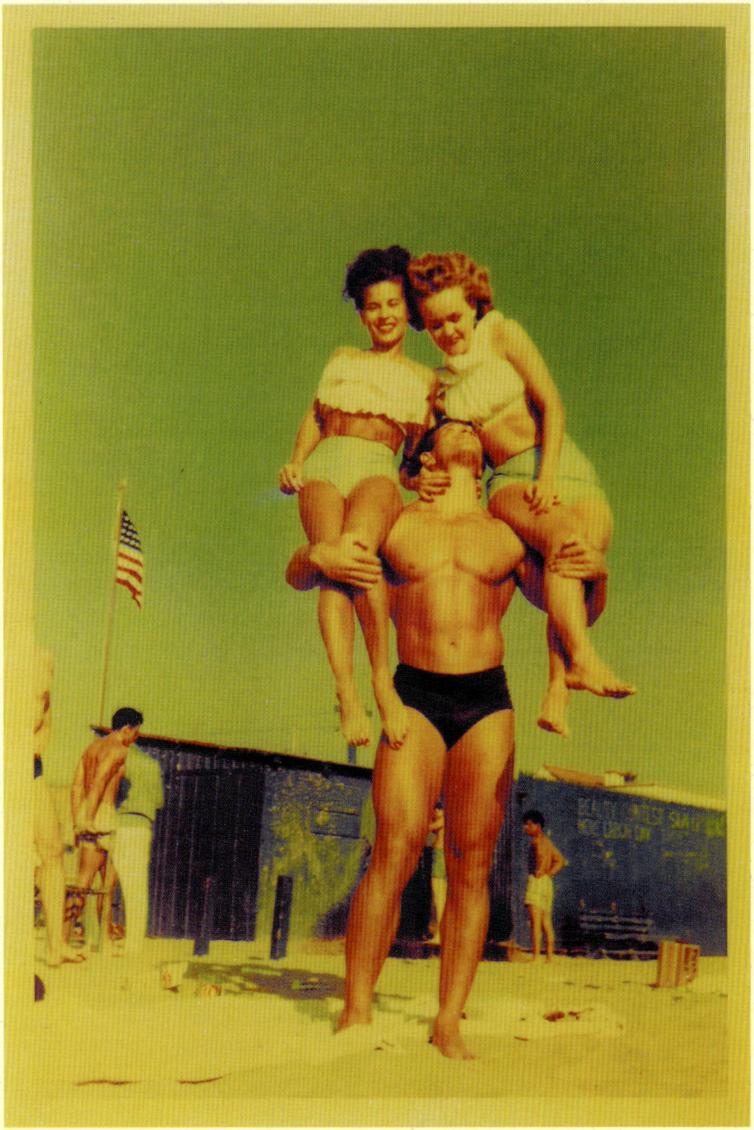

Bob McCune, Muscle Beach (?).
Unattributed snapshot, 1949.

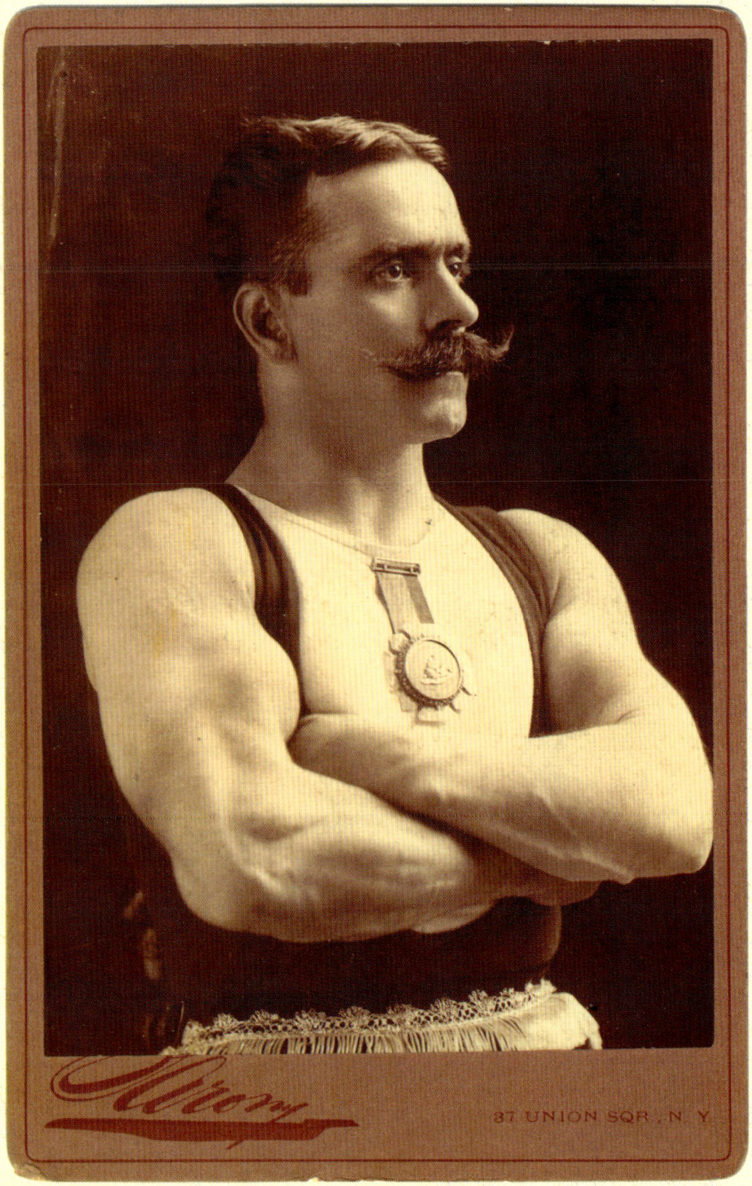

Charles A Sampson, Prussian strongman by Sarony, New York City. Cabinet card, c. 1895.

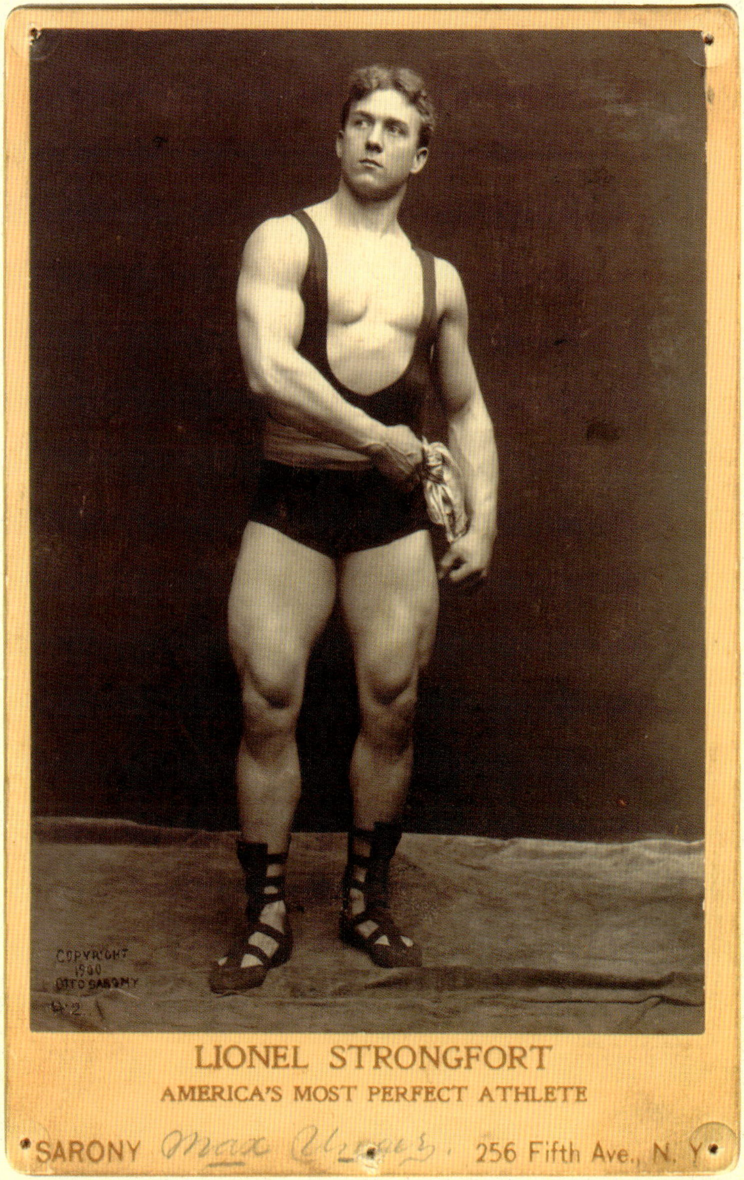

Lionel Strongfort (Max Unger),
America's Most Perfect Athlete by Sarony,
New York City. Cabinet card, 1900.

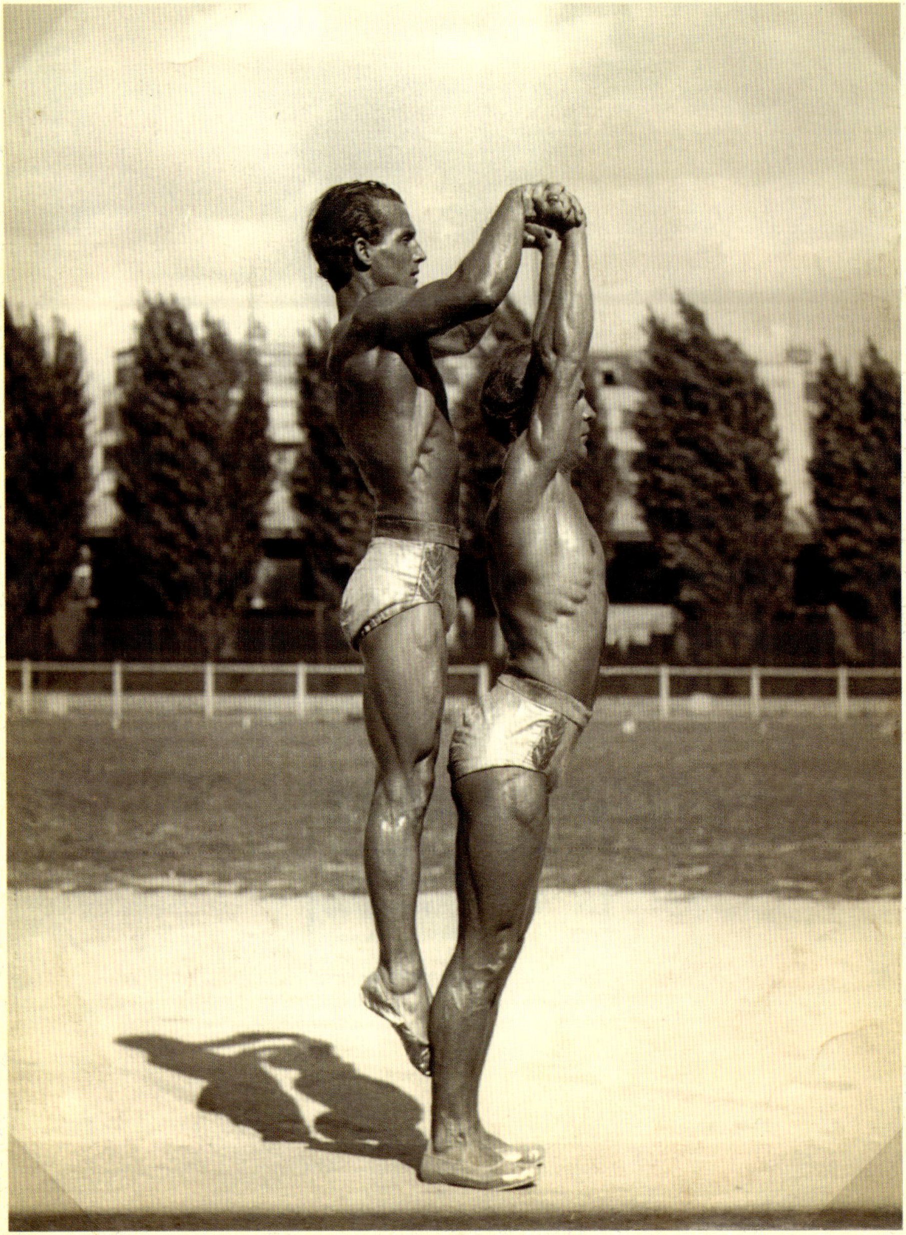

Unidentified French acrobats
by Adolphe Picoche. Silverprint, 1945.

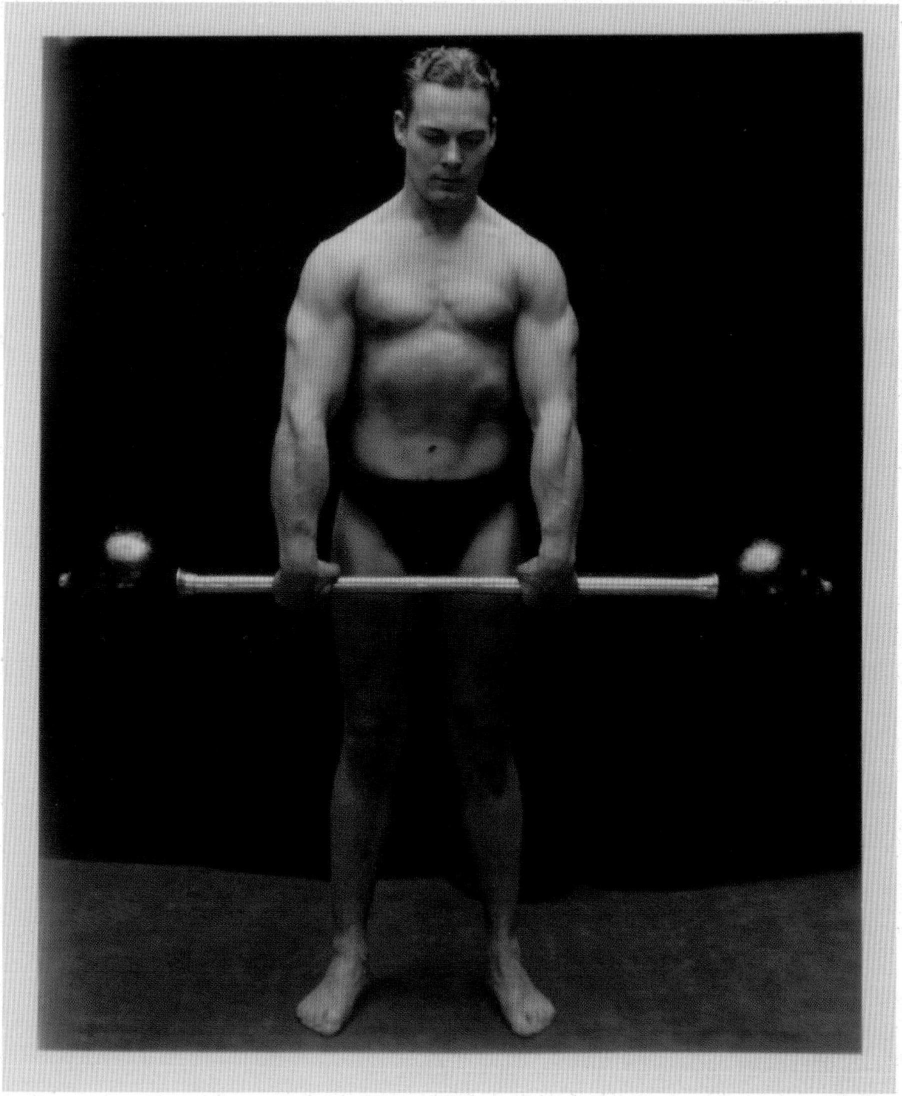

Charles Treadwell. Unattributed
American snapshot, c. 1925.

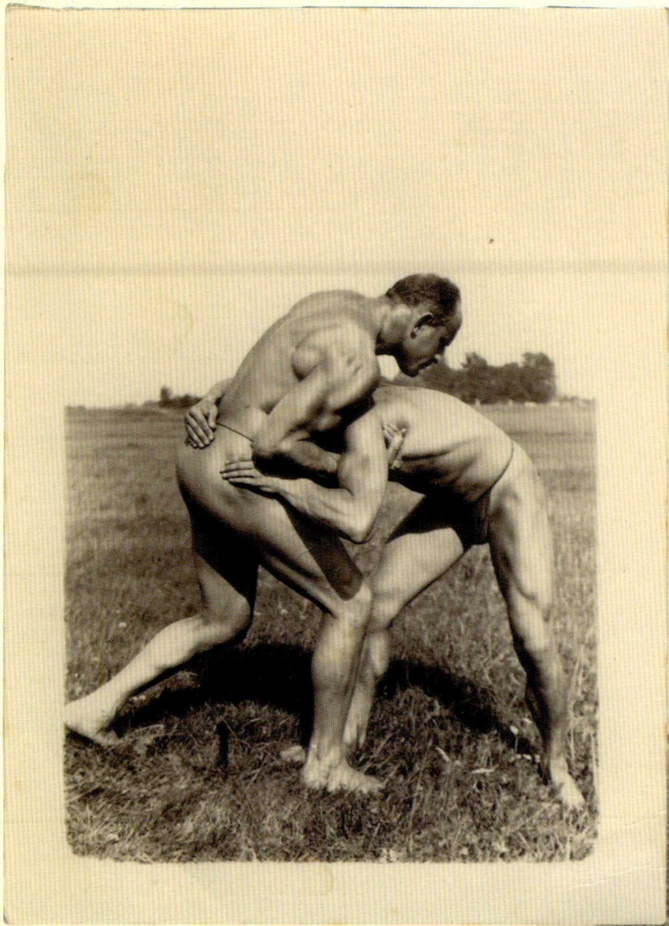

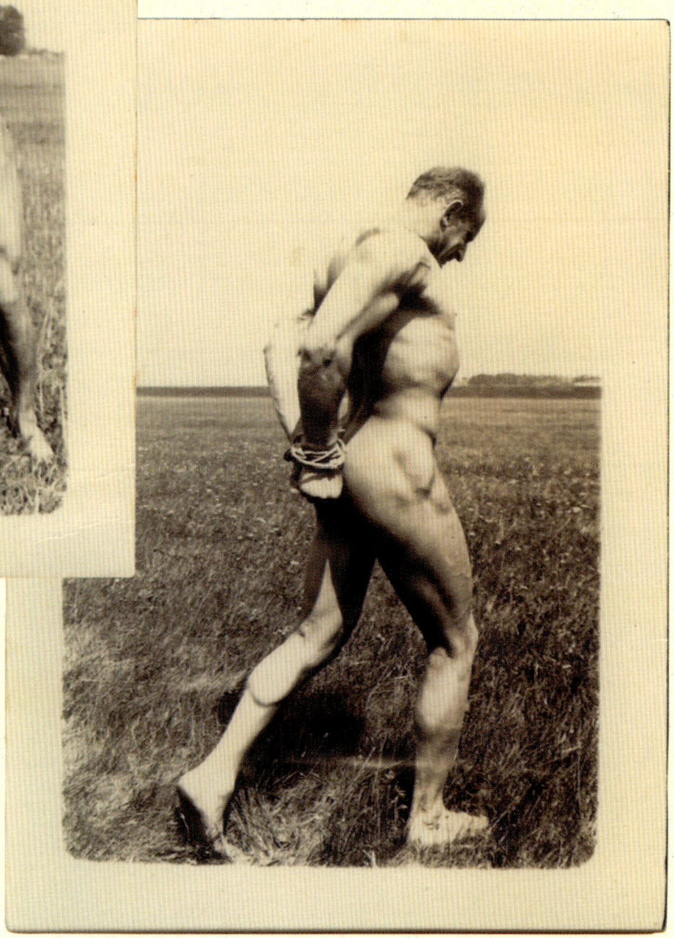

Anonymous snapshots, c. 1930.

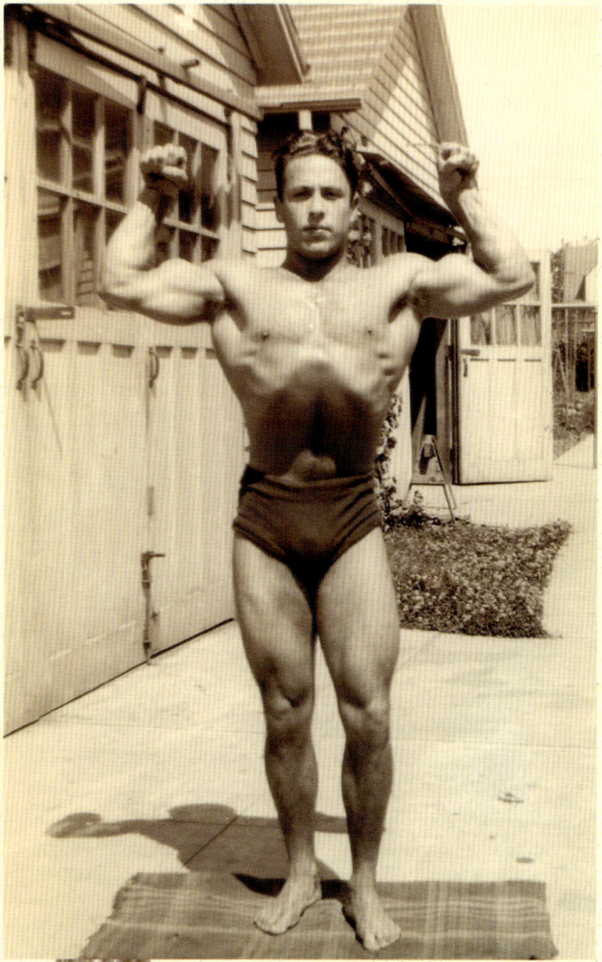

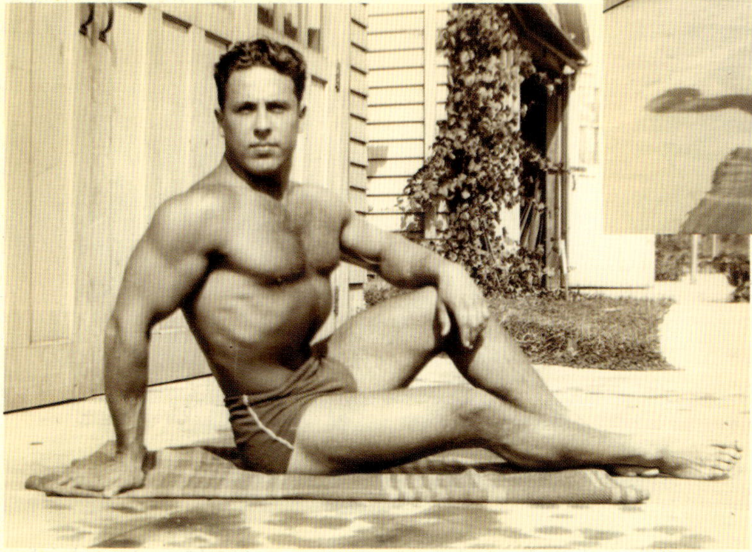

Sam Loprinzi, Portland, Ore.
Unattributed snapshots, 1936.

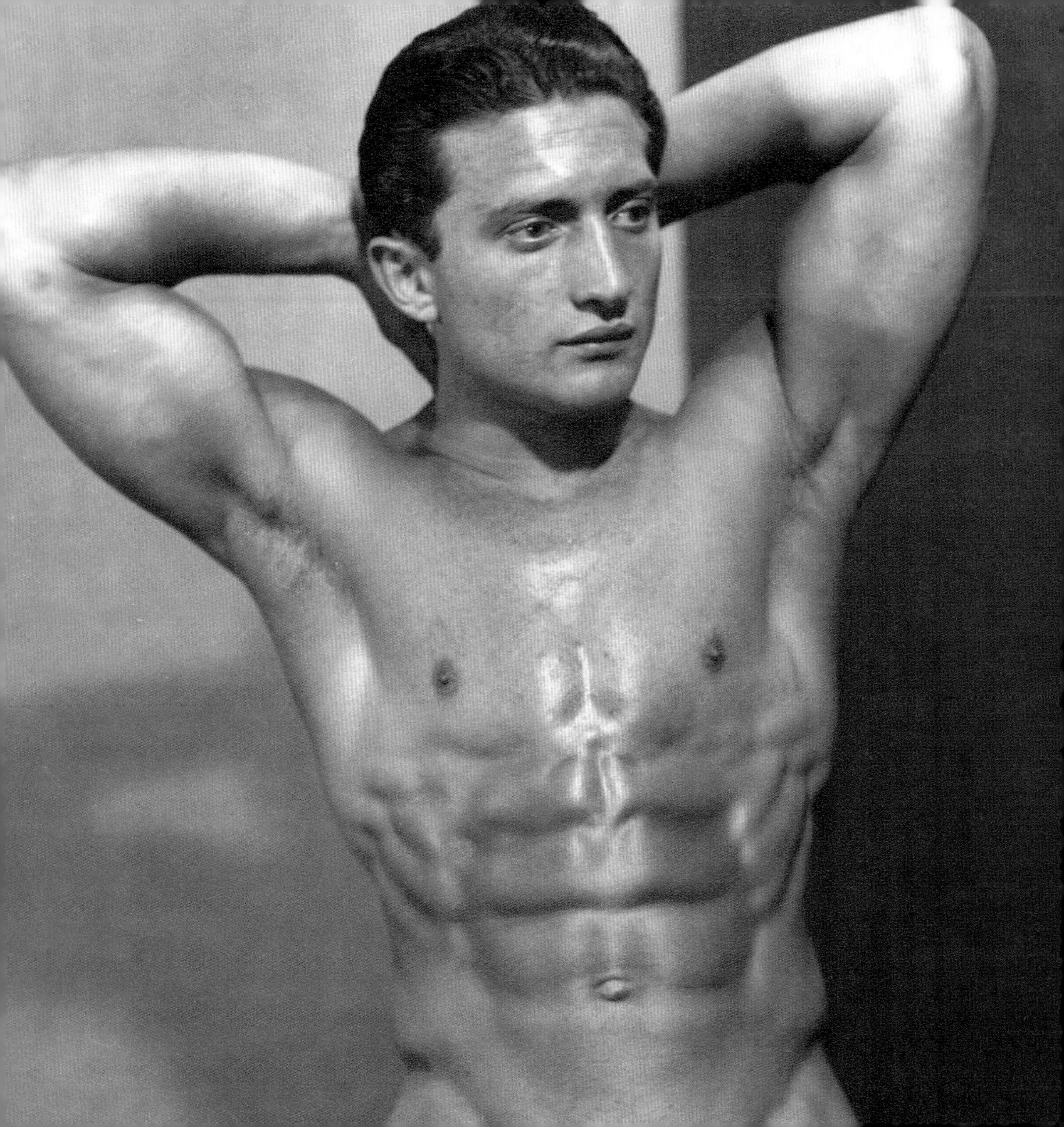

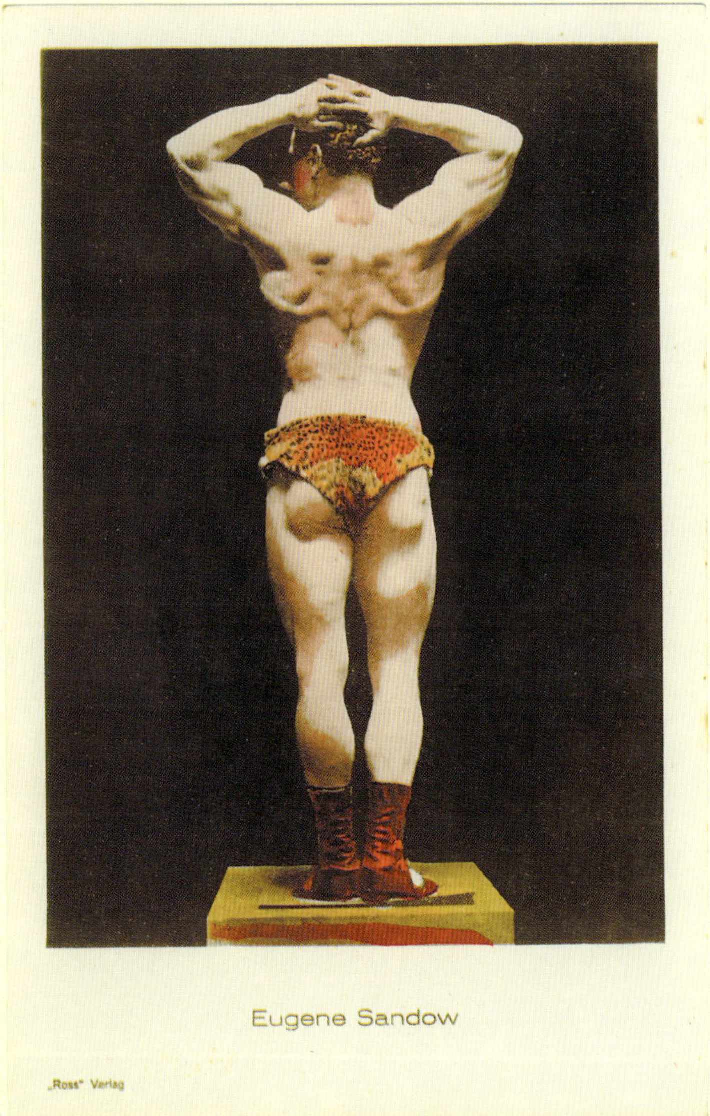

(Opposite) Unidentified model
by Earl Forbes. Silverprint, c. 1940.
(Above) Eugen Sandow by D. Bernard, Melbourne.
German postcard, 1905.

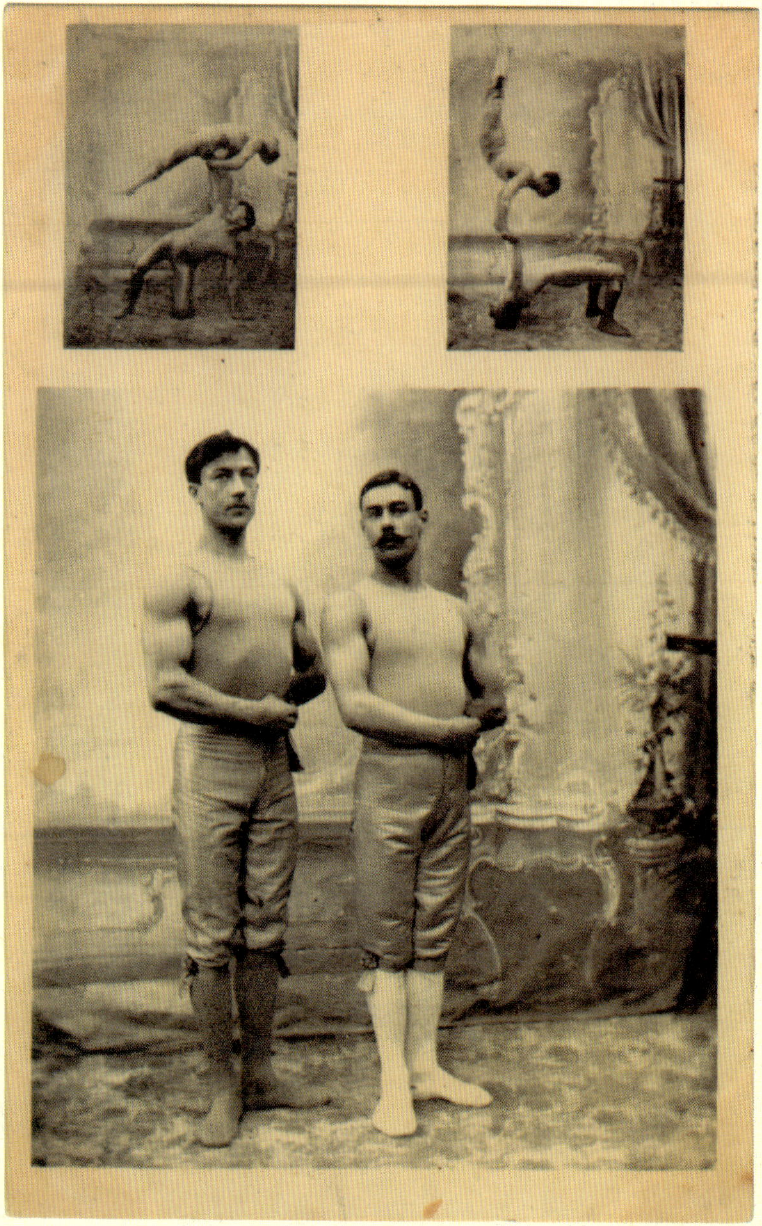

Anonymous hand-balancers.
Italian (?) postcard, c. 1920.

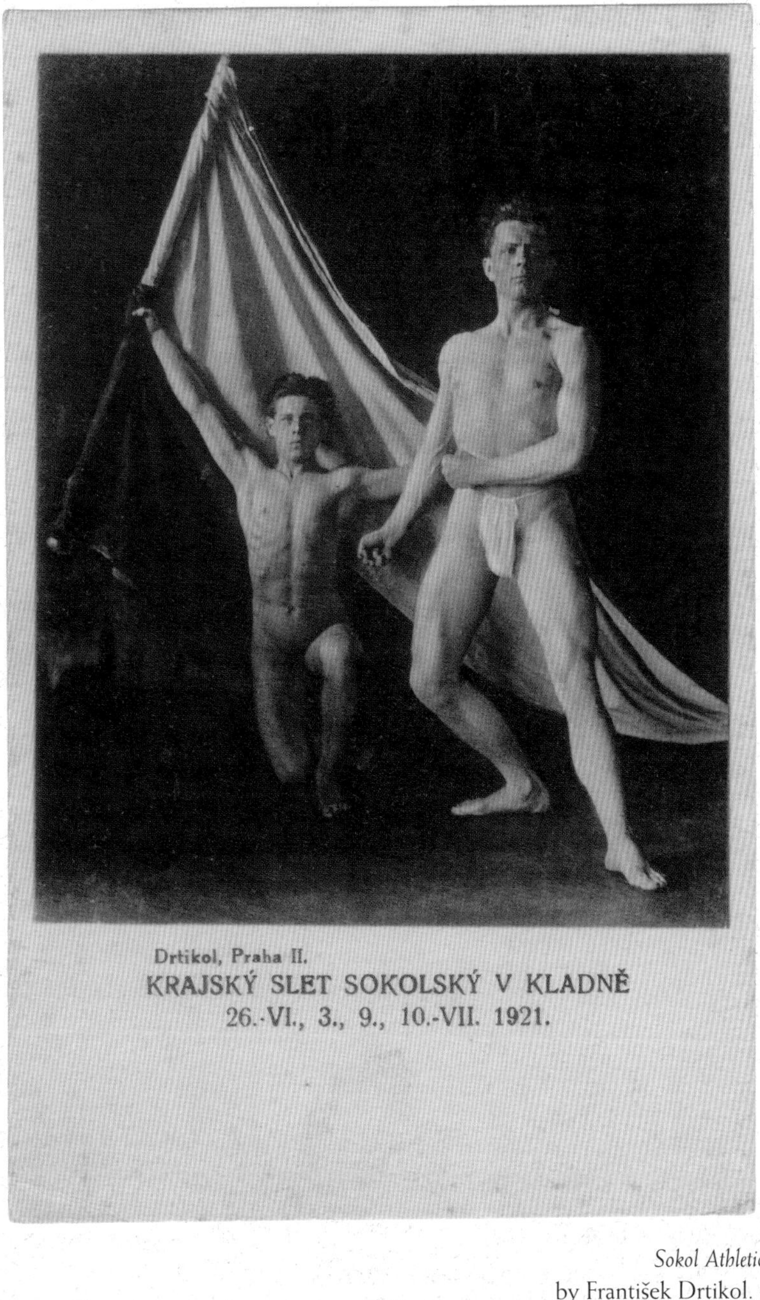

Sokol Athletic Games promotional image
by František Drtikol. Czech postcard, 1921.

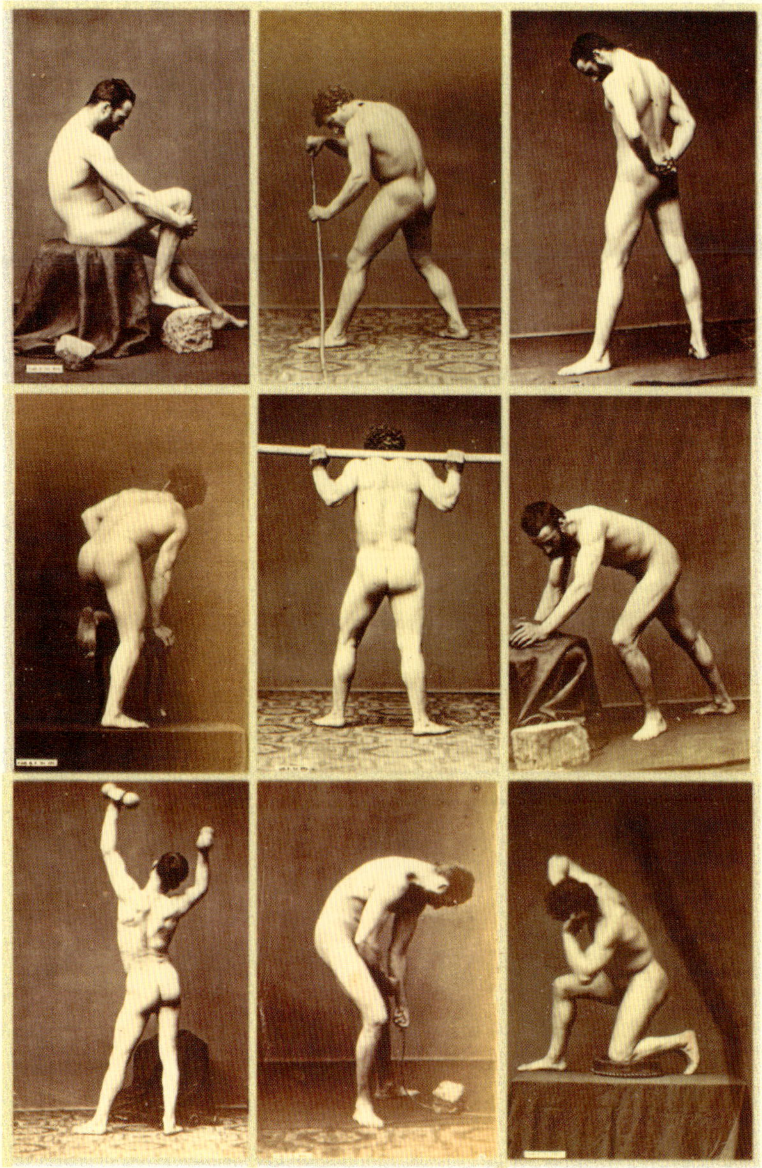

Studies for the use of artists, by A. Calavas, France. Albumen print, c. 1895.

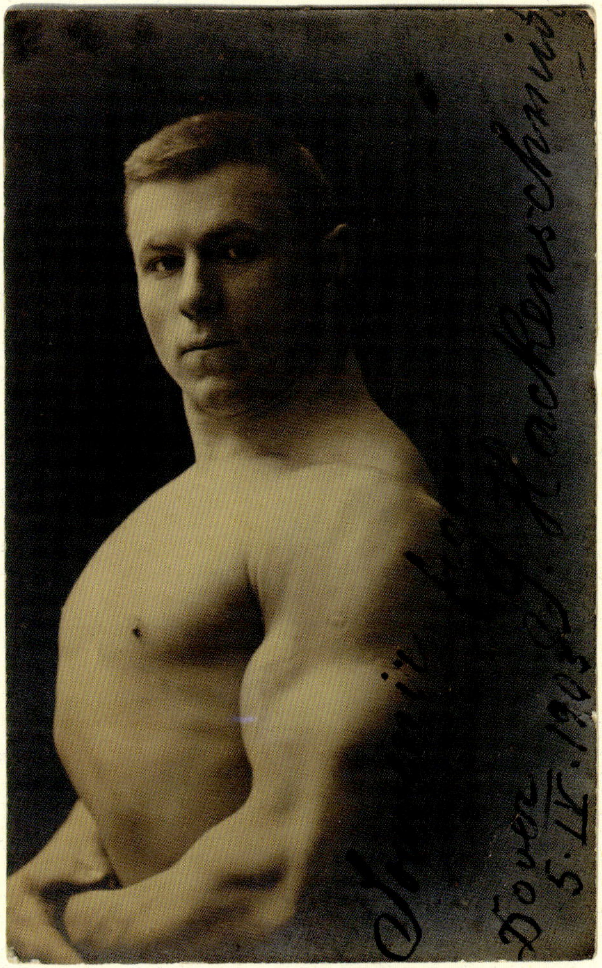

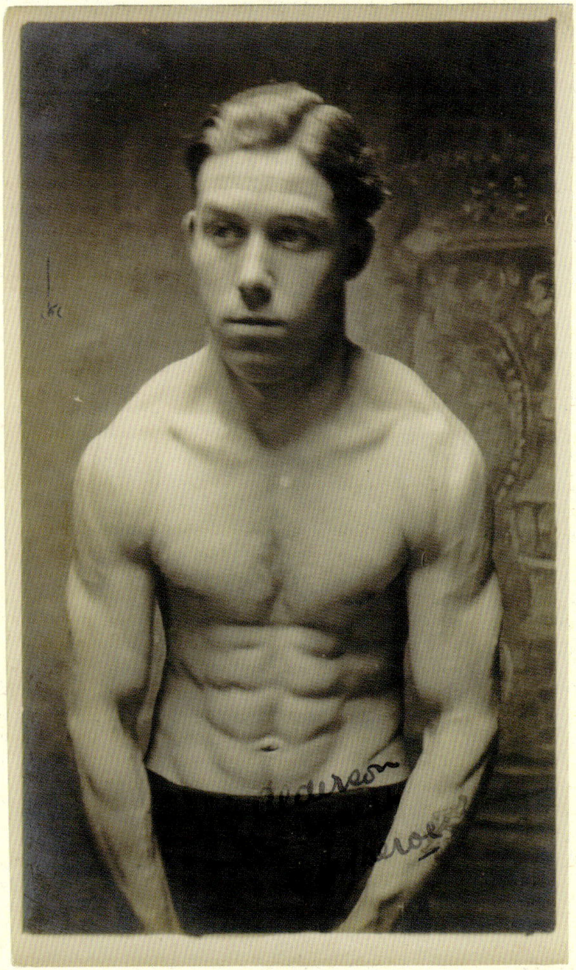

(Left) George Hackenschmidt, The Russian Lion; wrestler, strongman and author.
Unattributed cabinet card, 1903.
(Right) Vic Alderson, Physical Culture Expert.
Unattributed British postcard, c. 1930.

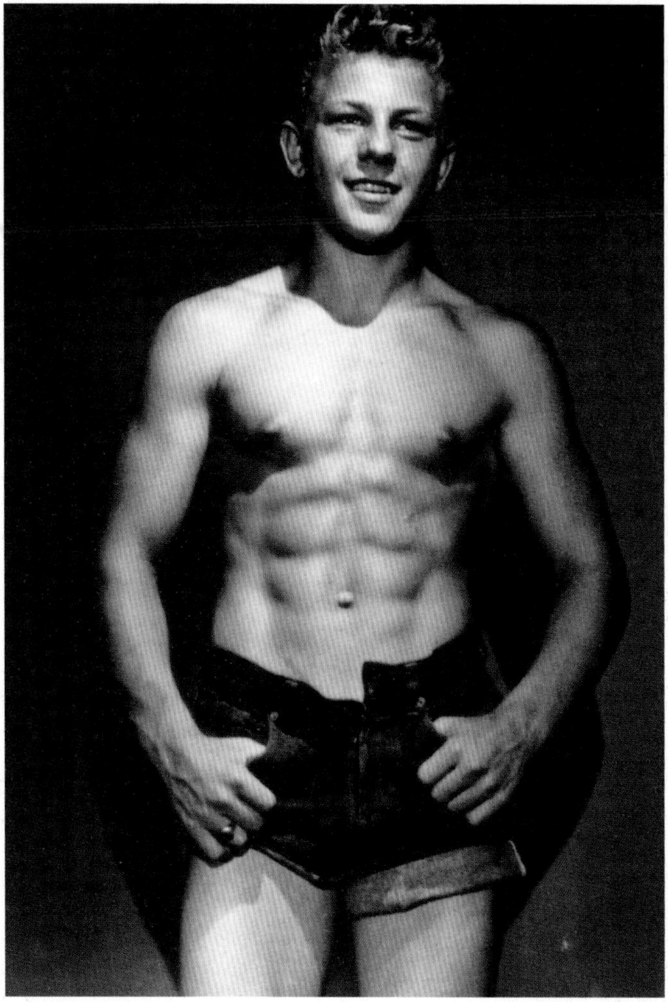

Rodger Vail by Eastern Model Associates.
Silverprint, c. 1954.

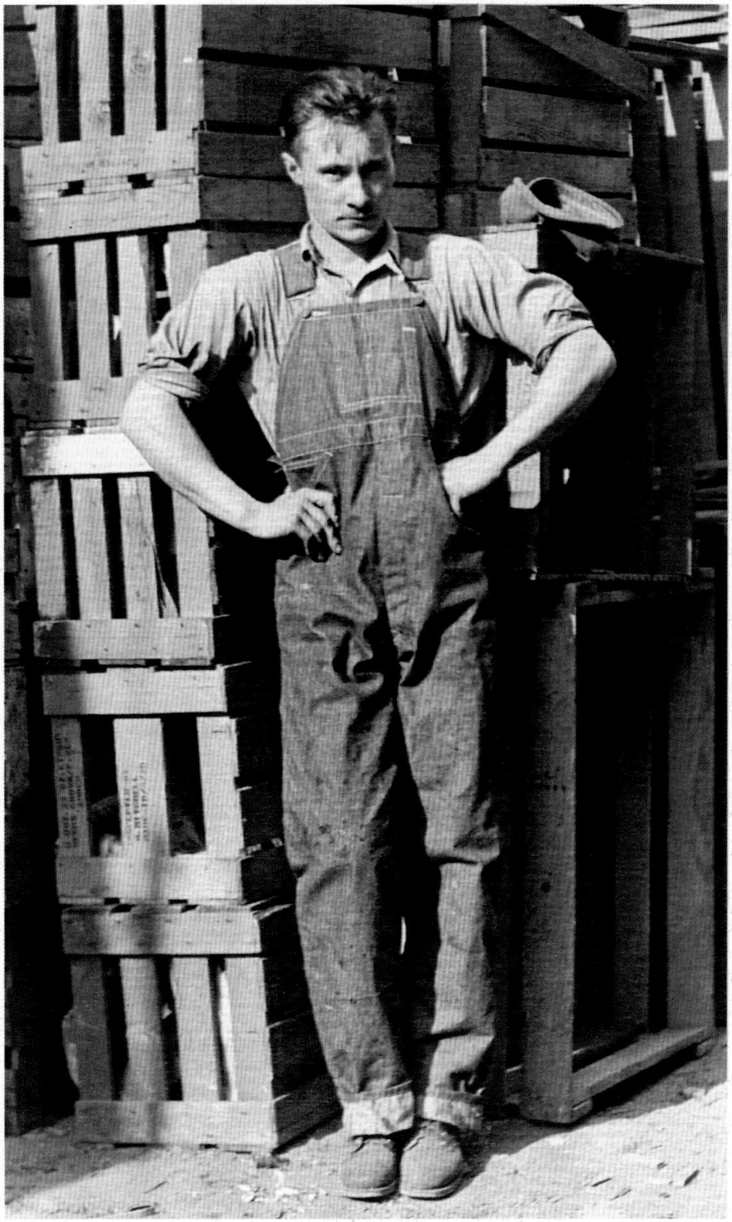

Anonymous silverprint, c. 1935.

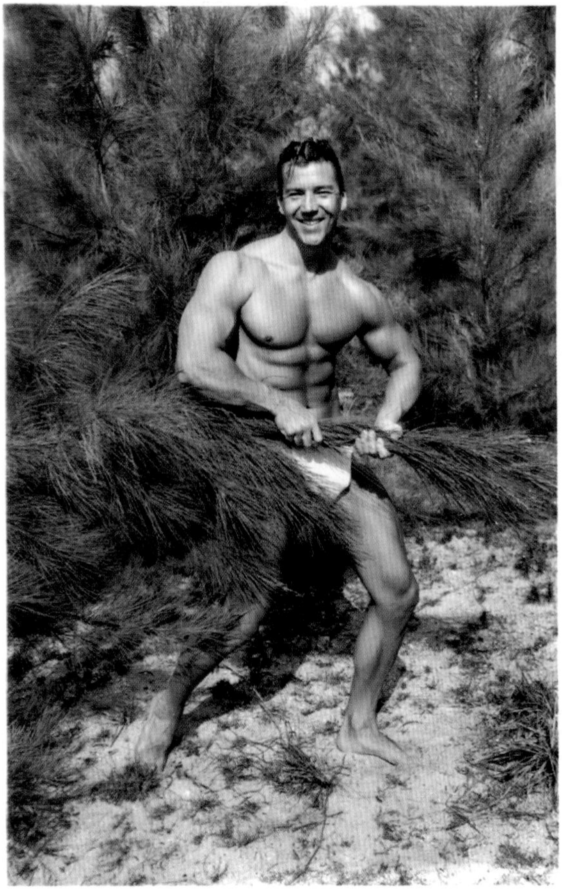

(Above) Mickey Hargitay, Mr. Universe 1955.
Unattributed silverprint, c. 1955.
(Opposite) Anonymous Russian snapshot,
c. 1920.

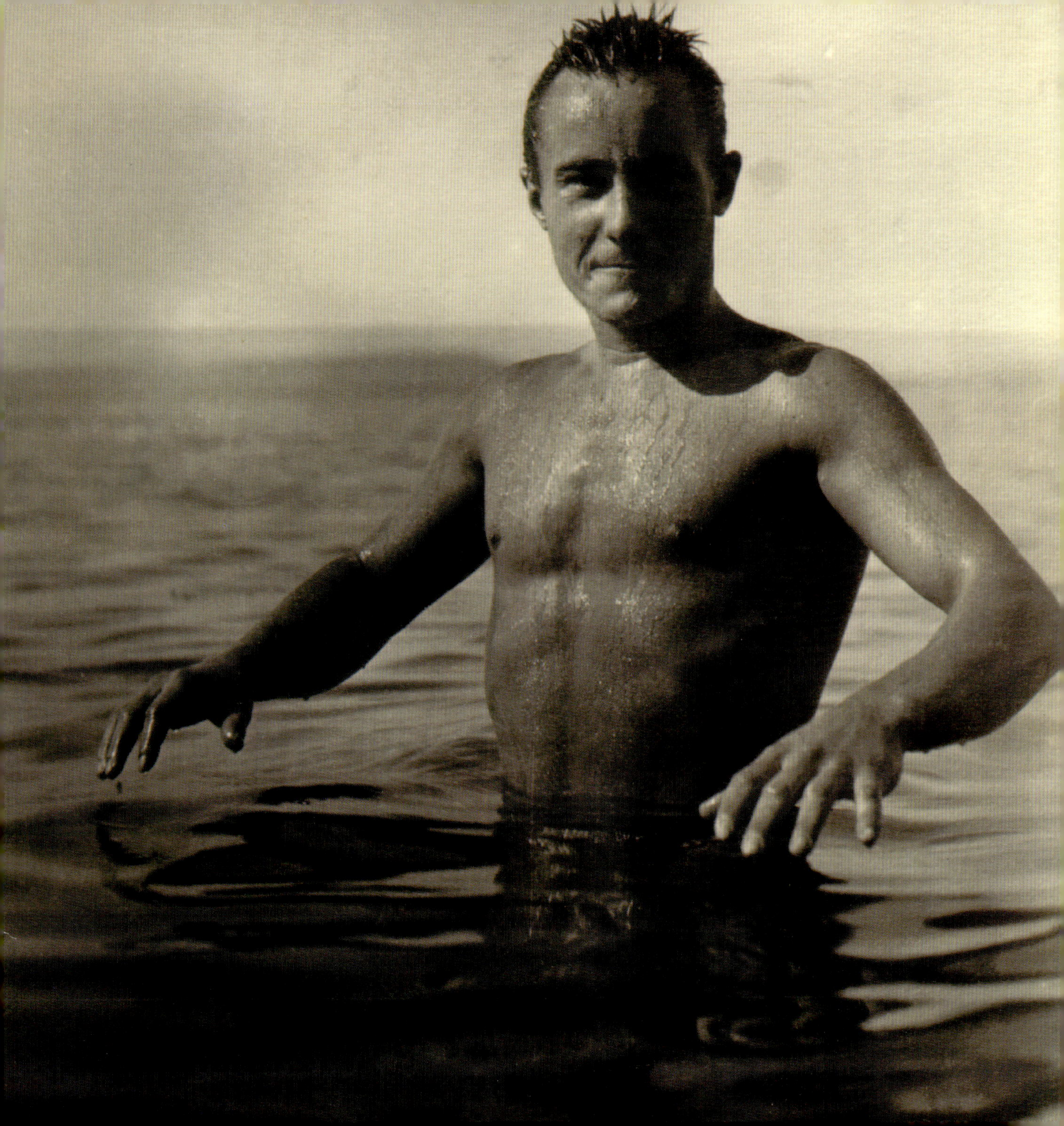

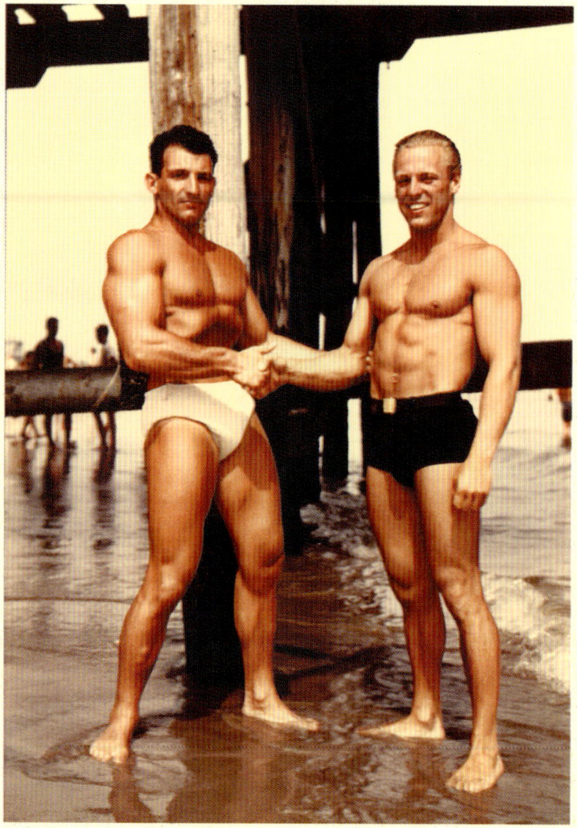

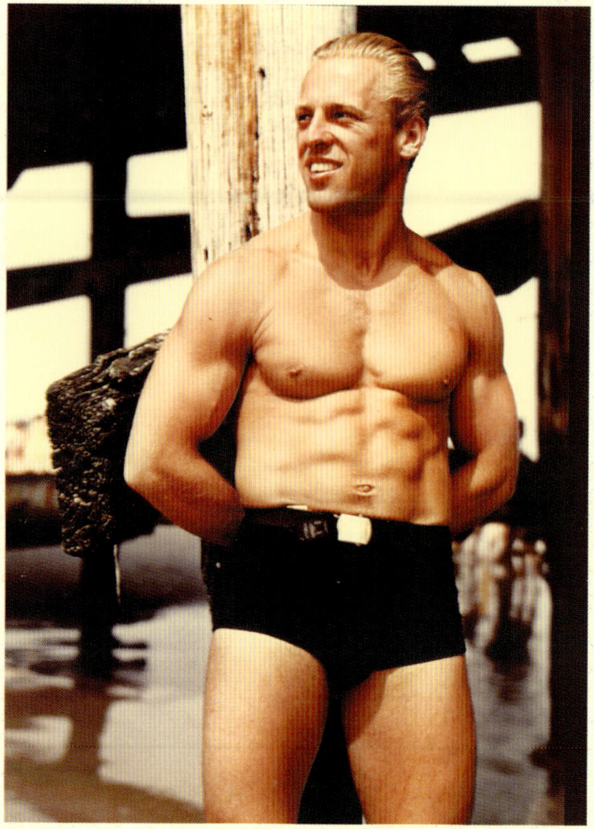

Everett Sinderoff and Henry Hojel
by Lon Hanagan. Color photos, c. 1945.

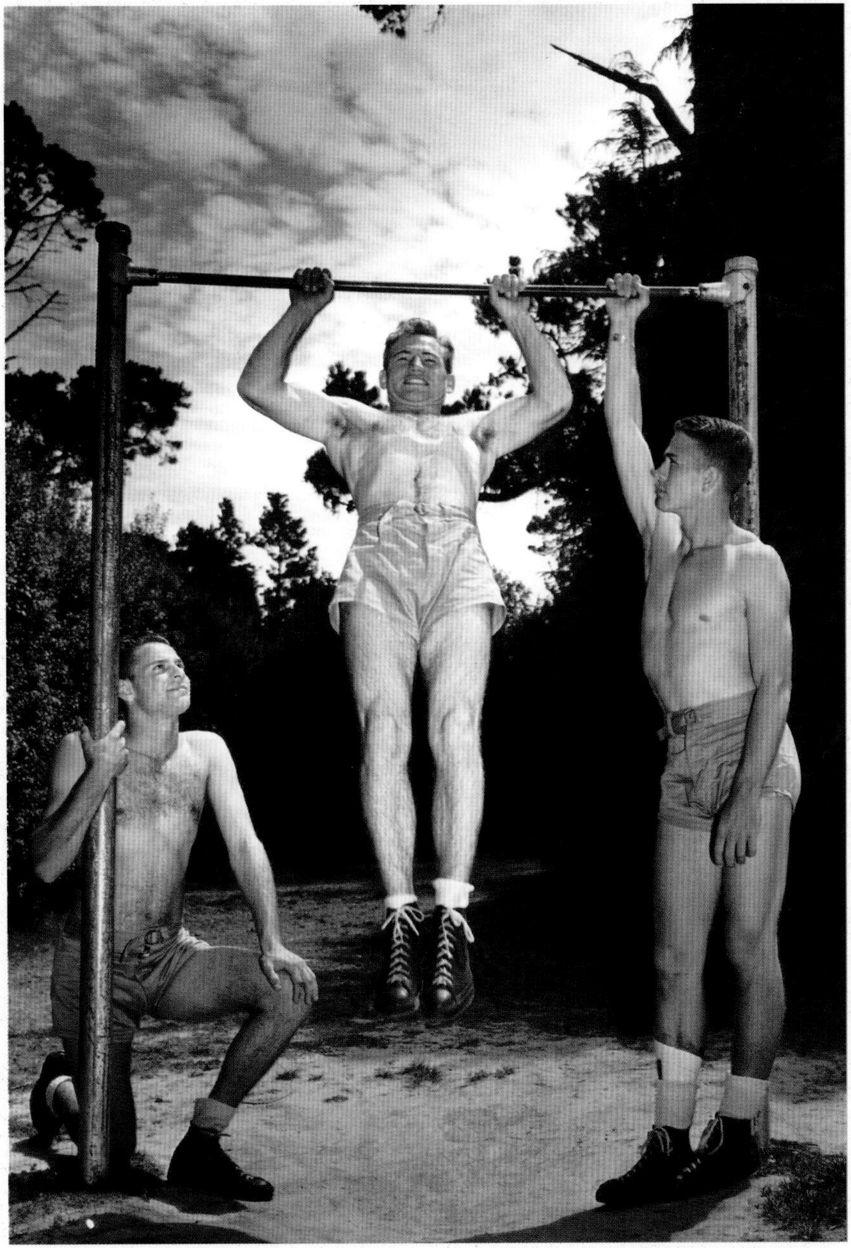

Military Exercise (or Civilian Conservation Corps). Unattributed silverprint, c. 1945.

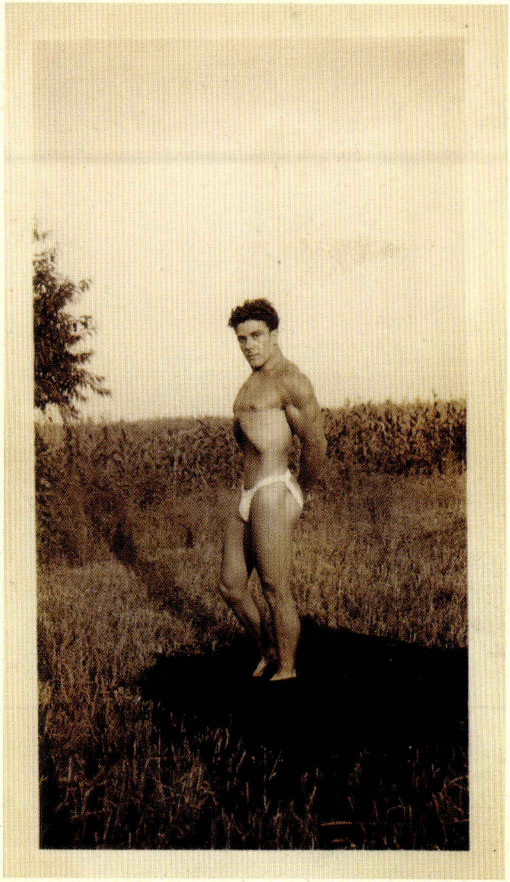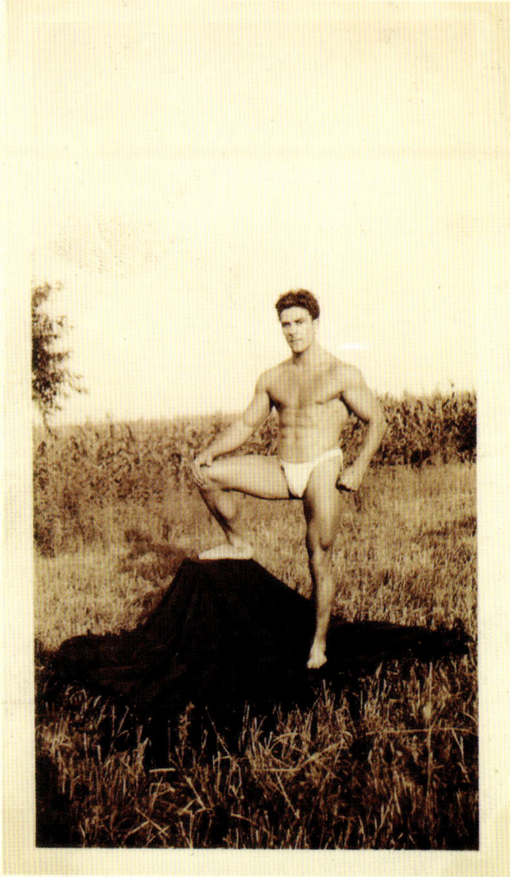

Mike Fontana.
Unattributed snapshots, c. 1930.

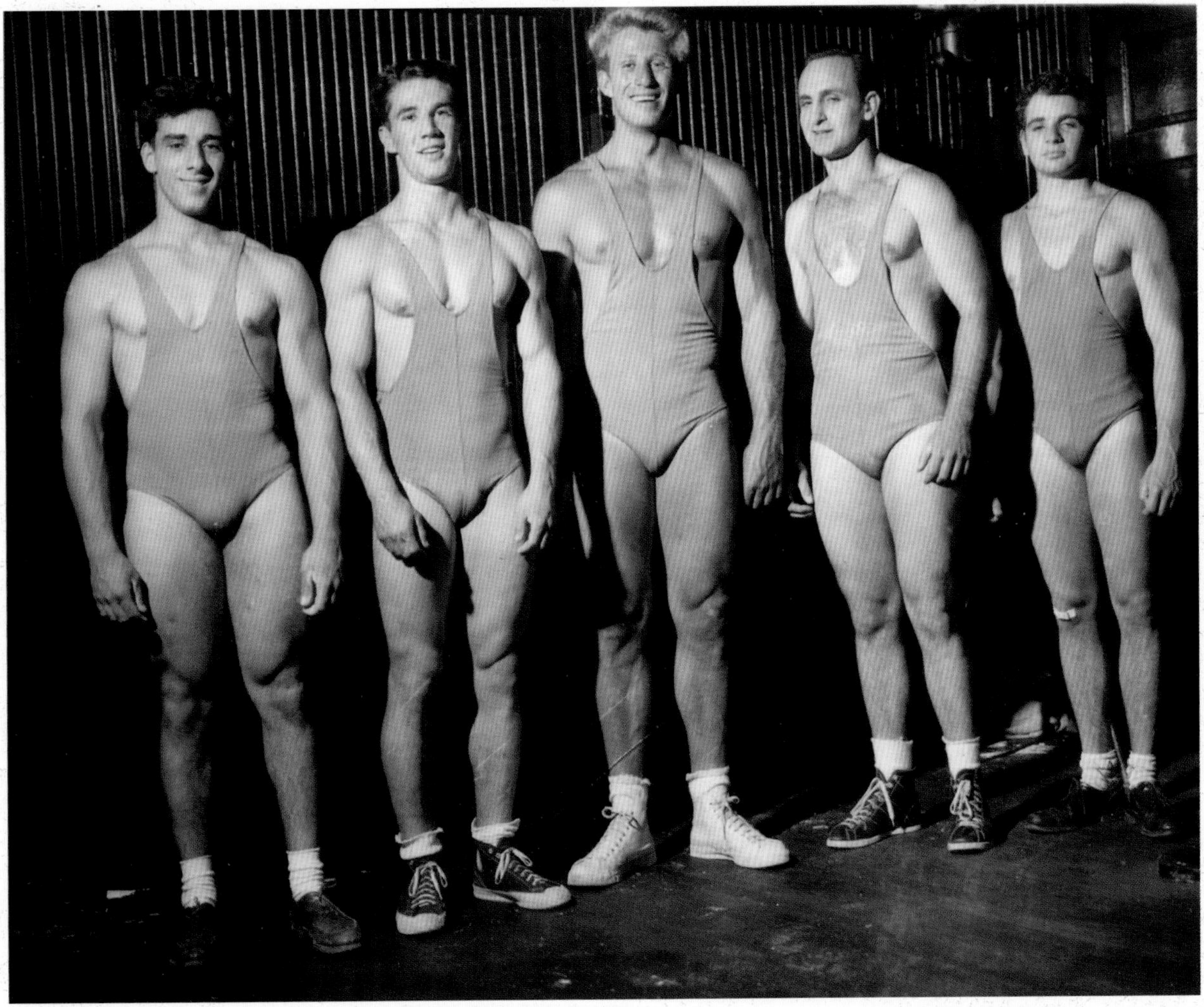

Weightlifters by Lon Hanagan.
Silverprint, c. 1950.

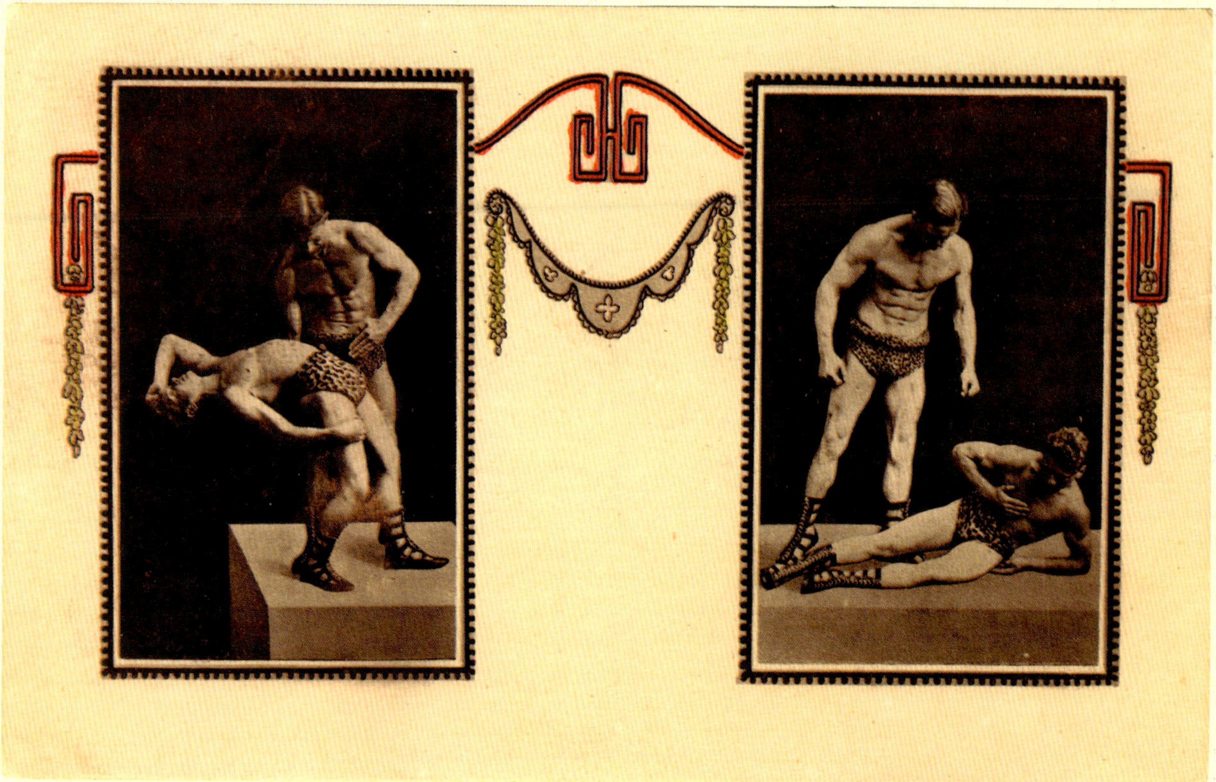

Anonymous postcard, published by Nordische Kunstanstalt, Ernst Schmidt & Co, Lübeck, c. 1915.

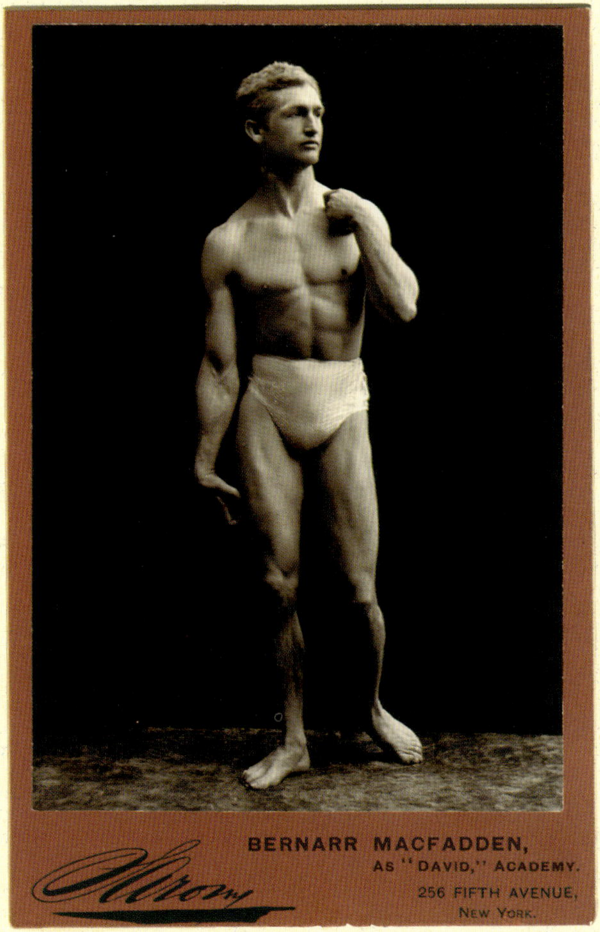

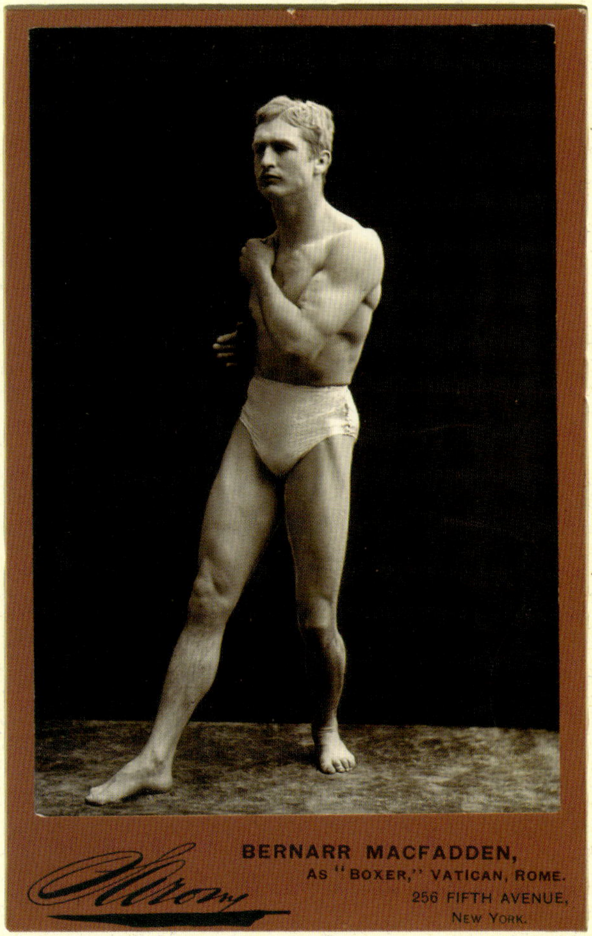

Bernarr Macfadden, publisher of Physical Culture Magazine, True Stories, *etc. in two* pose plastique *images,* from a series by Sarony, New York City. Cabinet cards, c. 1905.

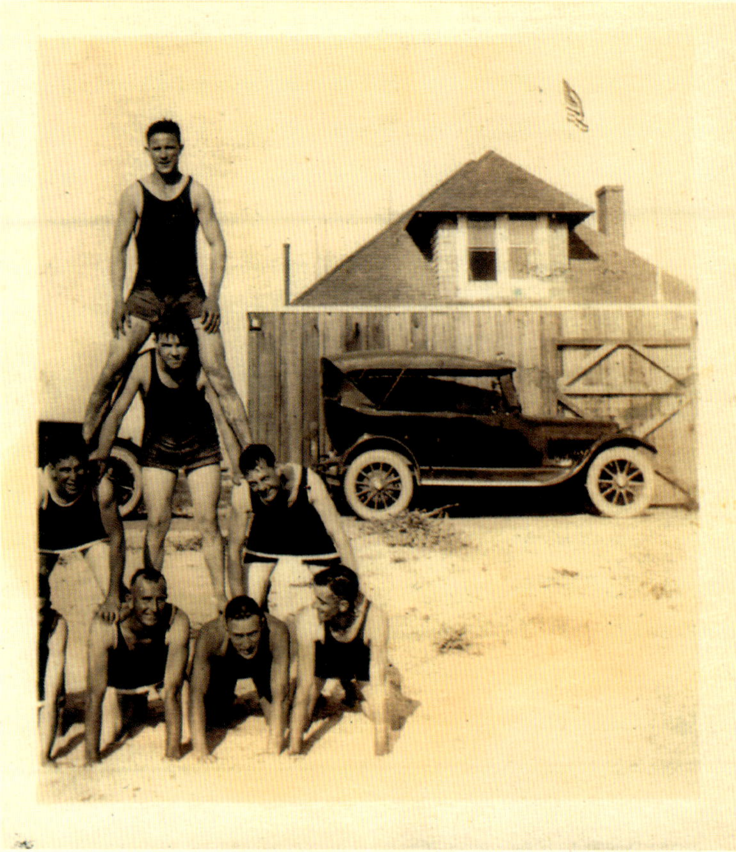

Snapshots by Carl S. Miller,
Indianapolis, Ind., c. 1914.

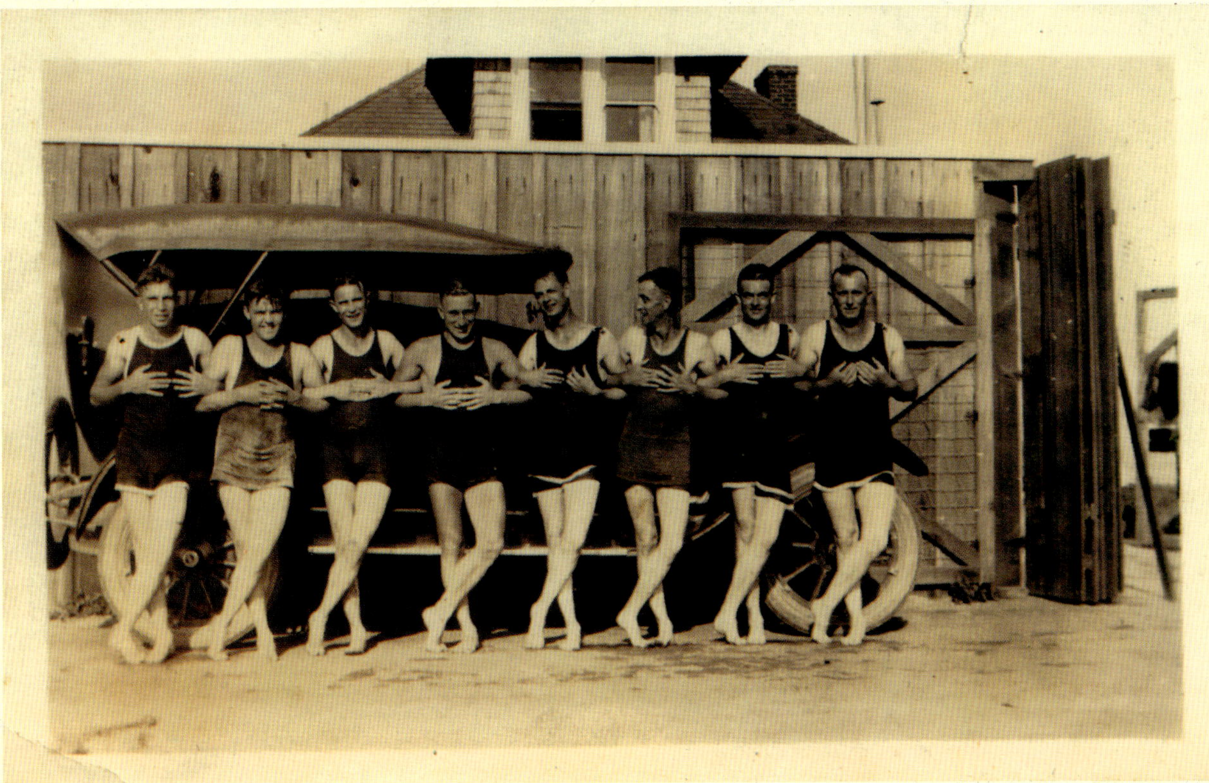

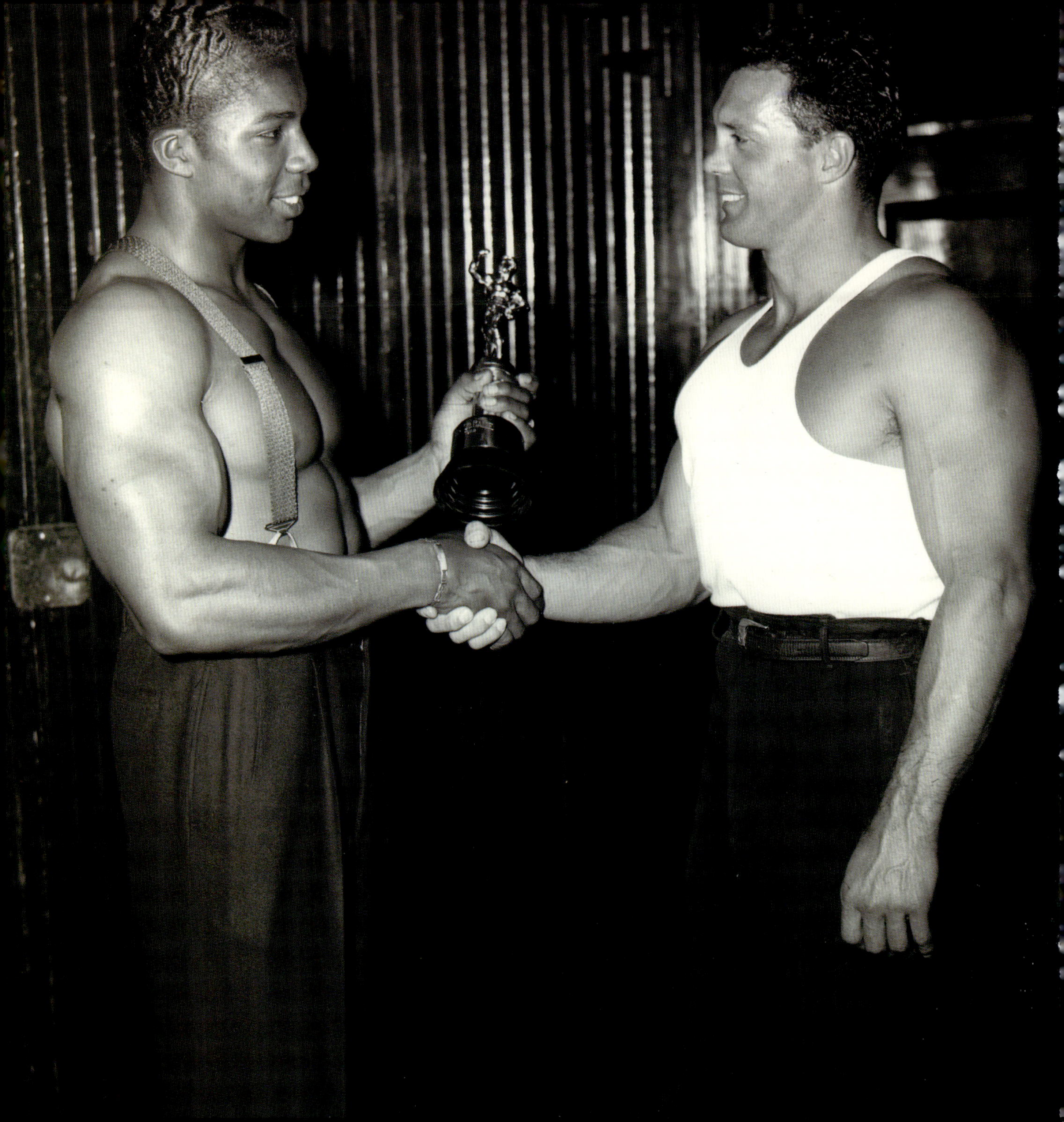

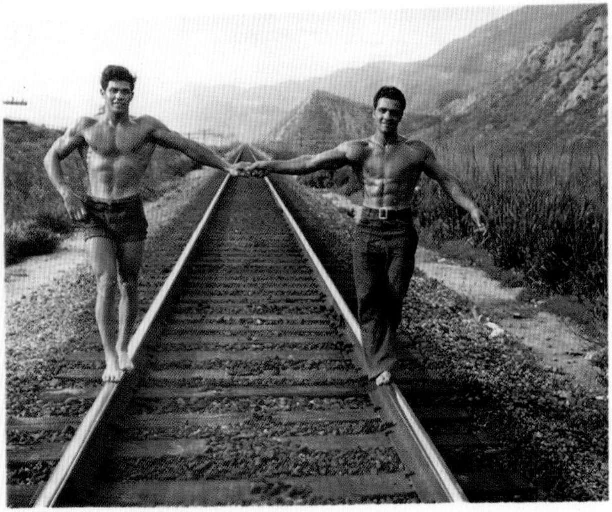

Acknowledgments

I wish to thank the following people for their help and encouragement on this project: Kevin Bentley, for his skills as both editor and friend; Melanie Haage, for her fine design; David Chapman, for generously reviewing the text; Reed Massengill, for his enthusiastic support; Mickey Hargitay, for kindly offering his remarks; Jules Bacon, for being both inspiration and contributor; and Trent Dunphy, my partner and fellow collector.

(Opposite) Bob Shealy and Vic Nicoletti
by Bruce Bellas. Silverprint, c. 1950.
(Above) Unidentified models
by Lon Hanagan. Silverprint, c. 1955.

For Trent

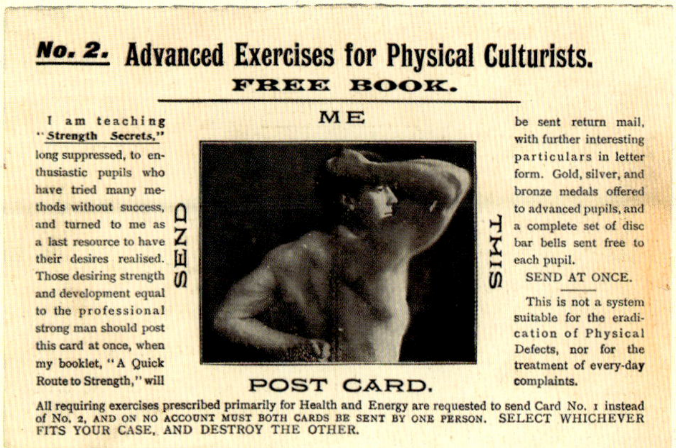

No. 2. Advanced Exercises for Physical Culturists.

FREE BOOK.

I am teaching "Strength Secrets," long suppressed, to enthusiastic pupils who have tried many methods without success, and turned to me as a last resource to have their desires realised. Those desiring strength and development equal to the professional strong man should post this card at once, when my booklet, "A Quick Route to Strength," will

SEND ME THIS POST CARD.

be sent return mail, with further interesting particulars in letter form. Gold, silver, and bronze medals offered to advanced pupils, and a complete set of disc bar bells sent free to each pupil.

SEND AT ONCE.

This is not a system suitable for the eradication of Physical Defects, nor for the treatment of every-day complaints.

All requiring exercises prescribed primarily for Health and Energy are requested to send Card No. 1 instead of No. 2, AND ON NO ACCOUNT MUST BOTH CARDS BE SENT BY ONE PERSON. SELECT WHICHEVER FITS YOUR CASE, AND DESTROY THE OTHER.

(Above) Thomas Inch, Britain's Strongest Man 1907, author and instructor. Promotional postcard, c. 1910.
Front cover: *A. Pitts*. Unidentified photographer. British postcard, c.1910.
Endpapers: *Czech Athletes* by R. Grunberger. Postcard, c. 1915.
Back cover: *Joffre L'Heureux, Canadian police chief.* Unattributed snapshot, 1949.

Council Oak Books, LLC
1290 Chestnut Street, Suite 2, San Francisco, CA 94109
1350 E. 15th Street, Tulsa, OK 74120

Book and jacket design by Melanie Haage

ISBN 1-57178-101-3
First edition / First printing.
Printed in South Korea.
01 02 03 04 05 06 5 4 3 2 1

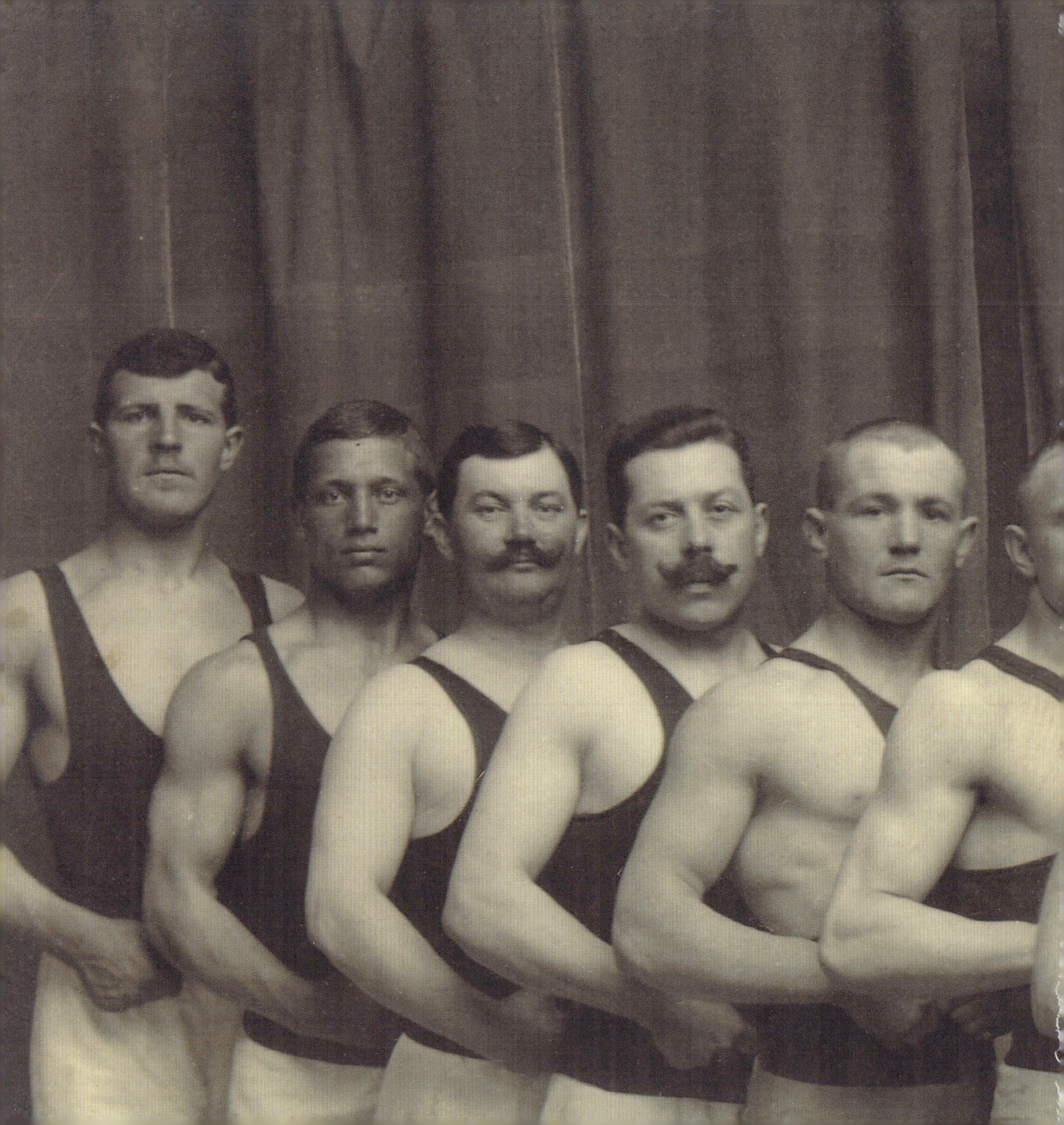